"*The Bible Out of the Pew* brings chten's considerable skills—the k......g..... ...... of a pastor, and the conversational style of a novelist. These have woven together a text that is deceptively easy to read and profoundly stirring to ponder."

—**Fran Leap**, Seton Hill University

"This thought-provoking volume, specifically addressed to the 'spiritual but not religious,' fosters appreciation of the Bible as a work of literature that prompts lively reflection on themes of enduring value and importance. Readers are likely to find that the Bible is much more complex, more diverse and self-critical in its witness, and far more interesting than they might have imagined!"

—**Frances Taylor Gench**, Union Presbyterian Seminary

"David von Schlichten offers a witty and wonderfully accessible introduction to the Bible that many, regardless of their religious affiliation or non-affiliation, will find enjoyable and enlightening. His dual roles as professor and pastor allow him to imbue this volume with wonderful insights into the Bible as well as a sensitivity to the everyday questions and concerns of those who encounter it."

—**Catherine Petrany**, Saint Vincent College

"David von Schlichten brings humor, kindness, and good sense, along with a thorough understanding of theology and the Bible, to *The Bible Out of the Pew*. Yes, it's useful for an introductory 'Bible as Literature' class, and yes, it's instructive for those who haven't studied the Good Book and are curious. But it's also thought-provoking to longtime Christians who want a deeper, less biased look at Scripture. Von Schlichten is funny and humble in addition to being quite learned, making the book a pleasure to read. It's easy to follow, with short chapters clearly laid out for the attention-challenged among us. Highly recommended."

—**Lee McClain**, Seton Hill University

The Bible Out of the Pew

The Bible *Out of the Pew*

An Empowering Guide
for the Spiritual
But Not Religious

David von Schlichten

RESOURCE *Publications* · Eugene, Oregon

THE BIBLE OUT OF THE PEW
An Empowering Guide for the Spiritual But Not Religious

Resource Publications
An Imprint of Wipf and Stock Publishers
199 W. 8th Ave., Suite 3
Eugene, OR 97401

www.wipfandstock.com

PAPERBACK ISBN: 978-1-5326-9651-0
HARDCOVER ISBN: 978-1-5326-9652-7
EBOOK ISBN: 978-1-5326-9653-4

Manufactured in the U.S.A.   09/19/19

For Bonnie, who said she'd be interested in a book like this.
We miss you.

And for Mle, who I hope will benefit from this.
I love being your opa.

Contents

Topic Six: The Epistles

Acknowledgements

Since books are always communal efforts (even when written in solitude), I have many to thank. First, thank you to my students, particularly those in my Bible as Literature class, who have guided me toward writing this book and have given me feedback on it. In fact, in general, thanks to the marvelous students at Seton Hill University. I love you dearly and hope you find this book helpful. It's written with you uppermost in my mind.

Second, thank you to Dr. Michael Arnzen, who suggested a book along these lines. For that matter, thank you to my wise and kind colleagues at Seton Hill. I am ever grateful for your brilliance, concern for the common good, and camaraderie.

I am also grateful to the people of Saint James Evangelical Lutheran Church in Youngstown, PA (not Ohio!), where I served as a pastor for seventeen years before becoming a professor full-time. Frequently, I look back with a deep sense that I failed you, but you have always been kind and generous. My time with you has had a significant positive impact on this book.

I offer a special note of gratitude to Seton Hill University's MFA Program in Writing Popular Fiction, which I completed on January 9, 2019. While this book is not a work of fiction, much of what I learned from the program about writing, publishing, and promotion applies here. The guidance of Dr. Lee McClain and Sharon Short has been especially valuable, as has the wisdom of my steadiest critique partners from the program, Kylie Peters and

Katie Catanzarite-Fitzpatrick, as well as Stacey Rubin and my latest critique partner, Kendra McConnell.

Thank you with all my heart to Mother Seton and the Sisters of Charity of Saint Joseph, who have inspired and shaped me in the best way as a professor and person. Hazard yet forward.

I am ever appreciative of the smart and generous people at Wipf and Stock for believing in this book and helping to bring it to the light of publication.

Thank you to Dr. Brené Brown, whom I have never met (yet) but whose work helped me to have the courage to lay aside my shame and be vulnerable enough to publish this book. I am daring greatly.

I am most appreciative of the following readers: Alfred Ruggiero (my stepdad), Mary Thomas, Nicole Holland, Paige Devlin, Rebecca Davis-Nord, and Victoria Adams. Your critiques and encouragement were helpful.

I also am grateful for Casey, Morgan, and all the delightful people at Barnes and Noble in Greensburg, PA, where I sat in the café and wrote much of this book. You were ever hospitable as I paced around the store, typed away on my computer, and drank an absurd quantity of tea.

And, as always, I am ecstatic about the love I receive from my stepdad, Alfred, and my siblings: Susan, Cyndi, and Peter (Mom, we miss you. You would have liked this book.). I also mention with love Glenn Canner, a *de facto* brother and so much more.

In addition, thank you to my sister-in-law Bonnie Keahilihau, who thought this would be a good idea for a book. I am sad that you are not alive to read it.

Finally, I overflow with gratitude for my wife, Kim; my children, Michael and Katie; my granddaughter, Mle; as well as the cats and Seaira the greyhound.

Without love, I couldn't write a word. No one can.

Day One: Introduction

I'm Interested in the Bible,
But Don't Cram Your Religion Down My Throat!

I promise I won't. Sharing religious views can be valuable, but pressuring people about religion is generally unkind and counterproductive.

Instead, in this book, we will spend forty-five days walking through the Bible. My goal will not be to convert you to Judaism or Christianity or even to believing in God. If you are a Jew or Christian, fine. You will find this book beneficial. But if you are some other religion or agnostic or atheist or your beliefs vary depending on the day, that's all fine, too.

This book is for the spiritual but not religious, that is, those of you who have some desire to nourish your spiritual side but do not want to identify with a particular religion. Some of you believe in God, some of you don't (yes, you can be spiritual without believing in God). Some of you may lean toward a religion, such as Christianity, but you do not attend worship regularly. You want to cultivate your spirituality, and you are open to the world's great sacred texts, including the Bible, but you are not interested in someone forcing a religion on you.

Unfortunately, among many of us religion professionals, there has been much disdain toward spiritual but not religious folks. We have complained that such people show a lack of commitment when it comes to religion. We have also noted that differentiating between spirituality and religion is a false dichotomy: one can be religious *and* spiritual, and many spiritual practices, such as yoga and mediation, are derived from religions.

While there is some validity to these points and while I used to be one of those annoyed religion professionals, my attitude has grown more positive toward those of you who are spiritual but not religious. As a result of my twenty-two years as a pastor and five years as a full-time religious studies professor, I understand more deeply that many of you designate yourself as such because you have found organized religion lacking. I am sympathetic; I have found it lacking, too, even while finding it beneficial. We in organized religion have made many horrible mistakes, and few things irritate me more than an obnoxious, closed minded, self-righteous Christian. What those of you who are spiritual but not religious are generally saying is, "My spiritual side is important to me, but my experience of religion has been largely negative, so I'm looking elsewhere." I get that.

This book is first and foremost for you. I want to introduce you to the Bible, but I have zero interest in trying to convert you to a religion.

Full disclosure: I am a pastor of the Evangelical Lutheran Church in America, a mainline Protestant denomination. I am well versed in the Lutheran Confessions and teachings such as justification by grace through faith, the priesthood of all believers, and the law/gospel dialectic. I also teach at a Catholic university and have found much in Roman Catholicism to be nourishing, such as Catholic social teaching and learning about some of the Catholic Church's extraordinary members, especially Saint Elizabeth Ann Seton and the American Sisters of Charity of Saint Joseph. However, this is not a book on Lutheranism or Roman Catholicism, and I am not the least bit interested in trying to win you over to either of those denominations or any other. It's up to you to decide what religion you want to practice, if any.

No, over the next forty-five days, my goal is twofold. First, I want to introduce you to the basics of the Bible. There is a notion among at least some Christians that the Bible is this handy-dandy, user-friendly, how-to guide for a great life. I wish! The Bible is a rich and fascinating book that rewards the patient reader, but handy-dandy and user-friendly it is not, nor is it a how-to guide for a great life. Truth is, the Bible is complicated and messy, and, in spots, it is bewildering and even offensive. Sometimes, after reading a passage, I think, "Ugh, I wish we could cut that out of the Bible," or "I have no idea what that means." I will give you the basics so that you can make better sense of the Bible. By the end of the forty-five days, you will be much more confident when it comes to reading and talking about this extraordinary book.

One of the benefits of knowing more about the Bible is that you can have better responses to those who reference it. America is full of people who toss around Bible verses or declare that the Bible says this or that. How's a person supposed to know who is referencing the Bible correctly? This book will be an invaluable start.

My second goal is to introduce you to ideas and stories in the Bible that are of value even if you do not believe in God. A good example is the book of Jonah. You know, the story with the whale (or whatever that creature is; it actually doesn't matter). As we will see, anyone, including atheists, can find that book both enjoyable (it's a hoot) and instructive. Each day, I will lift up a passage in the Bible that has something in it of value regardless of a person's view of religion or God. Obviously God is central to the Bible, and I don't mean to ignore that fact. I have just learned that, to a point at least, there are parts of the Bible that can be of use for almost anyone.

Most of us have found this to be the case when it comes to works from other religions. For example, when we read Greco-Roman mythology, we generally don't believe that the gods and goddesses of Olympus are real (although you never know; I'm praying that Athena's real), but that fact doesn't mean that I don't find the stories about them enjoyable and instructive. The same goes for the deities of ancient Egypt, the Norse gods and goddesses, and so on. I learn much from the *Bhagavad Gita* even though I don't believe in the god Krishna. On and on we can go. I don't need to buy into the religion behind a great literary work in order to enjoy and learn from it.

If you believe in the God of the Bible, great! I mean no disrespect. I am not here to deflate your faith. My point simply is that, at least to an extent, a person can gain much from the Bible even without practicing the religions based on it.

Here's how we'll proceed. Each day, I will recommend a short reading from the Bible, so you should get yourself a copy. Then I will provide background on the passage in question. Next, I'll offer discussion questions and topics that you can ponder alone or with another person or a group. Finally, I'll suggest a short bottom line to provide a conclusion.

By the way, if you are using this as a text for a college class, and if your semester is the usual fifteen weeks long, then you have three sections per week, a very manageable amount of reading for your students. Just a suggestion.

The translation I will reference is the New Revised Standard Version, or NRSV for short, but you can use whatever translation you want. Some of the more reliable ones are the New American Bible (Revised Edition) and the New International Version. Of course, you can use the good ole King James Version, but, while it is lovely literarily, it is difficult to follow. There is a New King James Version that is basically the same but with some updated language. There is also a delightful and thought-provoking paraphrase of the Bible called *The Message* that is easy to follow, but remember that it is a paraphrase, not a translation, which means that it doesn't follow the original languages, Hebrew and Greek (and a little Aramaic), as closely as a translation does. If you don't have a Bible, you can reference the whole thing at biblegateway.com.

The Bible is divided into what are called "books," and each book is comprised of chapters and verses. For example, "Genesis 3:1–19" means the book of Genesis, the third chapter, verses one through nineteen. I will make my way through the books roughly in the order in which they appear in the Bible. If you don't know where a book is, don't be afraid to use the Bible's table of contents (it puzzles me how often people don't think to do that).

By the way, I will not draw from every book in the Bible. I am just providing you with an introduction. If you want to read every book, go right ahead. Knock yourself out (figuratively, of course). Also, at the end of this book, I list resources for further study.

There are different editions of the Bible. For example, the Protestant edition has 66 books, while the Roman Catholic edition has 73, and some Orthodox editions have even more. The difference lies in what books are included in the Old Testament. So as to be as inclusive as possible, I will reference only books that are found in all editions, but doing this does not mean that I don't find value in the books I don't reference. It's all worth your attention. Remember, my work here is just an introduction.

Regarding dates, I will use the abbreviations BCE and CE, not BC and AD. BC and AD are oriented around Jesus. I mean no disrespect to Jesus, but I want this book to be as open as possible to people of all religions, so I am going with BCE and CE, which stand for Before the Common Era and the Common Era respectively, the Common Era being that which Jews and Christians share. Those abbreviations are used widely among us scholars. The dates themselves, though, don't change. BCE refers to the same time period as BC, and CE refers to the same time period as AD. For example, we can say that David reigned as king of Israel around the year 1000 BC or 1000 BCE. The two dates refer to the same year.

If I have just confused you, simply remember that BCE = BC and CE = AD. For example, at the time of my writing this, it is the year 2019 CE or AD.

The Old Testament/Hebrew Scriptures were originally written in, you guessed it, Hebrew (plus a little Aramaic, which is similar to Hebrew), while the Christian Scriptures/New Testament were written in Greek. So then, if I say, for example, "In the original Greek/Hebrew it says blah blah blah," you'll know what I'm talking about.

Two more points. One, since this is the Bible, obviously God is mentioned a lot. If you don't believe in God, then maybe you can think of God as a metaphor for Truth or Love, two traits that are central to God's nature. Or you can think of God as a character, just as you would think of, say, Athena as a character when reading the *Odyssey*.

Point number two is about language used to refer to God. The Bible tends to employ male language and pronouns for God. I follow that practice here for the sake of convenience, but understand that God transcends gender. Actually, in my personal devotions, I frequently use feminine language for God. Feel free to do the same. In the end, God is every gender and more.

All right, that's everything. Say a prayer (or don't), prepare to yoke the disparate, and let's go!

Part One

The Old Testament / Hebrew Scriptures

Day Two: The First Creation Story

D ay Two will be on that famous six-day creation account. We will get to that in a minute, but first, I need to provide some background that will carry you through the next several days.

Introduction to the
Old Testament/Hebrew Scriptures

The Bible is divided into two parts, the Old Testament and the New Testament. The Old Testament covers the story of Israel before the birth of Jesus. The New Testament covers the life of Jesus and the work of the early church. The Old Testament is also scripture for Jews and was such long before Jesus was born. Naturally, Jews, who generally do not believe that Jesus is the Messiah or God, do not call the Old Testament by that name but call it, usually, the Tanakh. It is also called the Hebrew Scriptures, as I have indicated. You might hear the term "Torah," which often refers to the first five books of the Tanakh. I am writing this book from a Christian perspective, but I mean to be respectful and open toward other religions, especially Judaism, from which Christianity came. From here on out, I will be calling the Old Testament by that term and not the Tanakh or the Hebrew Scriptures, but I wanted to highlight that, for millions of people, the Old Testament is the entirety of Scripture.

On a related note, I have often found that Christians tend to, well, "Christianize" the Old Testament, such as by seeing the characters as Christians or by seeing everything in the Old Testament as somehow prefiguring or prophesying Christ. Back in my parish ministry days, for example, I had a lovely elderly parishioner who, at my Bible studies, always called the people in the Old Testament "Christians," even after I corrected her. I knew her well enough to understand that she didn't mean any harm; she was just looking at the Old Testament through a Christian lens that she was incapable of removing.

In reality, though, little in the Old Testament has anything directly to do with Christ, and the characters certainly are not Christians. It makes about as much sense to call figures in the Old Testament Christians as it would to call the ancient Christians Democrats or Republicans. There were no members of either party back then because those categories didn't exist. Likewise, there were no Christians during the years before Christ. There are no Christians in the Old Testament, period.

So then, as we make our way through the Old Testament, I may mention Christ, but my focus will not be on Christ but on understanding the Old Testament on its own terms. I mean no disrespect to Christ, but the bottom line is that the Old Testament is much more than a lengthy introduction to Jesus.

Introduction to Genesis

Genesis, the Bible's first book, is about beginnings. The first eleven chapters deal with humanity in general, starting with creation, Adam and Eve, their sons Cain and Abel, followed by Noah and the Tower of Babel. Chapter 12 shifts to focusing on the people of Israel, who are known as the Hebrews, the Israelites, and, eventually, the Jews. In many ways, the Bible is about God's relationship, or covenant, with these people, whom the Bible identifies as God's chosen people and who have been promised a special land, called Canaan. Chapters 12–50 are about Abraham and Sarah, who are the parents of this great nation, and the first few generations of their descendants, ending with Joseph, one of their great-grandsons.

Tradition says that Moses wrote the book of Genesis, but most of us scholars think it is the result of several authors whose works were edited, or redacted (that's the lingo we tend to use in biblical studies), together.

Reading: Genesis 1

Background

Here we have the famous six-day account of creation. There has been endless debate about whether we should take this account literally or figuratively. You can discuss that if you want, but I would like to focus on what the story means and not on whether it happened exactly as reported.

This account of creation has some important features. One is that God makes everything alone. In the ancient world, most people believed that creation was the result of gods working together or killing each other or having sex or something involving more than one god. Not here. God does it all without assistance. Further, God creates through speaking. So we have God acting alone, and we have the power of God's words (and maybe the power of words in general).

Note, also, how much separating there is in the story. God separates day from night, light from dark, waters from waters, water from land.

After separating, God creates inhabitants. The sun, moon, and stars inhabit the sky. The sea creatures and fish inhabit the sea. The birds, the air. The animals and people, the land.

Next, we have God granting humans "dominion" over the rest of creation. You might want to consult multiple translations to see how this verse is rendered (Warning: translations always have a bias, even the beloved King James Version, which was written in part to support the British monarchy). People have long used this verse to justify human exploitation of the planet, but that understanding is faulty. Having dominion really means being a caretaker—"steward" is the (flawed) term we generally use in the church—not an abuser. Just as a good ruler who has dominion over a nation is supposed to care for and help her subjects, not abuse them, so also are people supposed to care for and help the rest of creation. Besides, doing otherwise is simply suicide for humanity (and just plain unfair toward the non-humans we share the planet with).

A final noteworthy feature of Genesis 1 is the establishment of the Sabbath, which, in the Bible, is sundown Friday to sundown Saturday (not Sunday; that's a later development). The central idea of the Sabbath is that it is to be a day of rest. It's also a day for focusing on worshipping God, but Genesis 1 emphasizes rest.

Discussion

Explore some of these themes that I lifted up from the chapter.

What role does separation play in the creative process? Generally, unity is a noble goal. We human beings, for instance, should work toward unity. But here is the idea that maybe division or separation is an important component to creation. What do you think?

Then God fills the separated areas with inhabitants. What do you make of that? What does that move suggest about the creative process?

Humanity's "dominion" over creation. How can we be better caretakers of the planet and its non-human inhabitants? This is an important topic even if you don't believe that humans are causing climate change. Isn't there something arrogant and just plain foolish about us humans hurting animals, plants, etc. for our own selfish gain? Besides, as Pope Francis points out in *Laudato si'*, it is often the case that, when we hurt the rest of creation, we wind up hurting ourselves, too, especially the poor.[1] Consider this topic and some concrete ways we can take better care of this fragile planet.

The Sabbath: We Americans are lousy about taking time for rest without feeling guilty. What do you think of the idea of a whole day for rest? Most of us complain that we are too busy, but don't we bring some of that misery upon ourselves? What if we said no to some of the mayhem and insisted on rest, even if doing

---

1. Pope Francis, *Laudato si'*, Chapter One, "What Is Happening to Our Common Home," Section V, "Global Inequality."

so means others will judge us? What if we stopped determining our self-worth based on how busy we are?

My wife and I have struggled with this concept. We are both hard workers, and, to an extent, we have both bought into the American tendency for people to define themselves primarily by what they do. Kim has admitted repeatedly that she has difficulty just sitting to watch TV because she then grows restless and feels guilty about not getting things done. I have an easier time just sitting, but still I derive a hefty chunk of my self-worth from my accomplishments.

The Sabbath is about *not* doing. It is about being, resting, focusing on God. Our society does not allow much time or permission to do something as "selfish" and "frivolous" as relax and contemplate something greater than yourself, but the concept of honoring the Sabbath calls us to do just that. What do you think of that idea? How are you at doing that?

My Suggested Bottom Line

Regardless of whether you take Genesis 1 literally or figuratively (or a combination of both), there are some great lessons and themes here that we can study together, such as about the creative process, taking care of creation, and Sabbath rest.

Day Three: The Second Creation Story

Reading: Genesis 2

Background

H ere we have what most of us scholars agree is a second creation story. In Genesis 1, God creates the world in six days. God creates all the animals and then humans, male and female. In Genesis 2, starting in the second half of verse four, we have the beginning of the second account: God creates man, then the animals, then woman. There are also differences in style and language in Genesis 2 that suggest that this is definitely another creation account and not a continuation of the account in Genesis 1. For example, in Chapter Two, God is called "YHWH" (usually translated as LORD, which is printed in small capital letters), but in Chapter One God is called "Elohim," translated as "God."

It is also in Genesis 2 that we learn the big rule: The man and woman can eat of any tree in the garden but not from the one in the middle of the garden. In stories, whenever you have a rule, you just know that, sooner or later, someone is going to break it.

Does it bother you that there are two contradictory accounts of the creation right next to each other in the Bible? In other words, do you take these stories literally or figuratively? If we take them literally, then it becomes a challenge to explain how two contradictory accounts of the same event can both be right. One suggestion has been that the second account simply goes into detail on the first and that the two stories, then, do not really contradict each other.

But there is nothing in the Bible that says that. The writer does not say, for example, "What follows in Chapter Two is an elaboration on what was described in Chapter One." Still, there are those who argue that the creation account in Genesis 2 is really a continuation of the account in Genesis 1.

Most of us scholars think that we simply have two traditions represented here. The point is not to describe literally what happened during creation but to share stories that help us to understand profound truths about God, the universe, and God's relationship with humanity.

Discussion

Let's explore this understanding found among many of us scholars that these are in fact two different creation accounts. Talk about them. What do they each say about God and humanity? How are their messages similar and different?

Also, what does it say about the Bible that there can be two different versions of the same event right next to each other? Incidentally, this is by no means the only time you will see this pattern. It is not unusual for the Bible to provide more than one account of the same event. The most obvious example is the four Gospels in the New Testament (Matthew, Mark, Luke, and John), each of which tells about the life of Jesus. The four accounts are roughly the same but disagree on key points. What do we make of these conflicting accounts?

Could it be that, by having contrasting versions, the Bible is allowing for diversity, at least to an extent? Is it built into the Bible that we don't have to agree on everything when it comes to God and spirituality? Of course, the Bible is not an "anything goes" book; there are standards, key narratives, and rules. But it has long seemed to me that the Bible allows room for difference and even disagreement.

I like that the two accounts don't quite match. There is something liberating about allowing for multiple viewpoints without trying to resolve them. But then, I have spent my life cultivating the ability to embrace multiple viewpoints, at least to an extent. For instance, if you asked me, "What's your religion?" I would say that, most of the time, I lean heavily toward Christianity. Specifically, being an ELCA Lutheran makes a lot of sense to me. But as a religious studies professor at a Roman Catholic university, I have grown in my receptivity to Roman Catholicism (for instance, every morning on my way to work, I pray the "Hail Mary."). I also am quite open to other religions and atheism. When I hear my fellow Christians incredulously declare, "Given how beautiful and amazing the world is, I don't know how anyone could possibly be an atheist," I find myself thinking, "It's really not that hard at least to be an agnostic. There is good reason to doubt God's existence, even though there is also good reason to believe in it. Sure, beautiful sunsets suggest that God exists, but widespread suffering greatly challenges the idea of God." All of that swirls around within me, even as I preach in a Lutheran church or reverently attend mass.

So having two different creation accounts that don't quite line up with each other is, frankly, no big deal for me. But that's just me. If that issue is a big deal for you, I certainly can understand. You are not alone, but I want to encourage you to worry less about resolving the differences. Perhaps worrying about differences says more about us readers than it does about the Bible.

What are your thoughts about these two accounts and what they say regarding God, creation, us, and the Bible in general?

My Suggested Bottom Line

There are two different accounts of the creation in the Bible, and that's a good thing because it suggests that we can have multiple perspectives and still be united.

Day Four: The Fall

Reading: Genesis 3

Background

"The Fall" is the term Christians use to refer to the story of Adam and Eve taking the forbidden fruit from the Tree of the Knowledge of Good Evil because, as a result of this sin, Adam, Eve, and all of creation fall from a state of grace into a state of sin, pain, and death. Because, according to the Bible, this event is the first sin, it is often called the Original Sin.

Fun fact: There is no concept of the Fall or Original Sin in Judaism or Islam.

This is one of those Bible stories that most people don't know as well as they think they do. We have heard this story—or at least some version of it—so many times, that we think we have it down. The devil comes to Eve in the form of a snake and tricks her into eating the apple, which she then gives to Adam. There is frequently the interpretation that Eve somehow deceives or seduces Adam into taking the fruit, that she uses her feminine wiles to lure him into sin. An underlying assumption to this understanding is that women are easily seduced by the devil and that they themselves are deceitful and seductive and that Adam never would have taken the apple otherwise because men are morally superior to women.

That interpretation, though, is nonsense.

I often show students a picture I stole (yes, I stole it; don't judge) from a children's Bible depicting the Fall. Eve is drawn with red lips and a heavy-lidded come-hither look. She is standing next to the serpent, who is wrapped around a tree, and she is holding an apple out to Adam, who is recoiling in horror. The message is clear: the woman is the evil seductress, while the man is the innocent victim.

There is so much wrong with this understanding of Genesis 3 that it's hard to know where to begin, but one of the most basic problems with this interpretation is that there is no basis for it in Genesis 3 itself. Never mind that there is nothing in the passage that identifies the serpent as the devil (it's just your average talking serpent), and never mind that there is nothing in the passage that identifies the forbidden fruit as an apple. Nothing in the passage whatsoever indicates that Eve seduces or deceives Adam into taking the fruit, and nothing indicates that Adam resists. After the serpent talks Eve into taking the fruit, she gives some to her husband "who was with her." Period. No seduction, no protest, no nothing. Readers have often suggested that Eve is easily led into temptation, while Adam is not. But actually, both Adam and Eve fall quite easily into doing the wrong thing.

Now, in the New Testament, in 1 Timothy 2:13–14, the writer declares that Eve was deceived and not Adam. I guess that's true in that the serpent entices Eve and never even talks to Adam, but with all due respect to the writer of 1 Timothy, Genesis 3 makes it clear that both man and woman are guilty. God certainly punishes both of them.

So keep in mind, as you discuss Genesis 3, that it is simply a misreading to conclude that women are more prone to sin or are seductresses or anything else that suggests that women are inferior to men. Even if the people in biblical times thought of women as inferior (and they did), it is absurd for us to think the same today. The evidence and logic say otherwise: women and men are equal.[1] Granted, men and women have some different attributes (although we are more alike than many of us want to admit), but

---

1. Indeed, identifying only two gender categories is simplistic, but, for the purposes of studying this passage, I'll just focus on man and woman here, since it is only man and woman who are mentioned.

being different is not the same as being superior or inferior. As human beings who have value and a right to live and pursue happiness, we are all equal, regardless of our gender.

We will see a lot of sexism in the Bible. I wish I could say otherwise. The good news is that we will also see parts of the Bible that undermine that sexism. And a given passage is still of great value (usually) even when it is sexist.

This issue of gender equity should be important to all of us, but it is of special interest to me because I grew up with an abusive biological father who was terrible to my mother and sisters. I resolved at an early age not to be like him, and I thank Goddess that I am not. I mean, I have his quirky sense of humor and love of cats and appreciation of the musical genius of Linda Ronstadt, but I did not carry on his sexism, racism, homophobia, and abusive behavior. Throughout my career, I have been particularly attentive to sexism and have been trying to move the needle closer to gender equity. Hence, I am involved in our local shelter for victims of gender-based violence, and I teach gender studies. My addressing of sexism in the Bible is part of my larger quest for gender equity.

The Bible's sexism is profoundly upsetting to me, but I do see much good in the Bible despite it. See if you agree.

Gender aside, one theme in this story of great value is that of over-reaching, excessive pride. That is what causes Adam and Eve to fall. They take from the fruit of the Tree of the Knowledge of Good and Evil. That phrase, "knowledge of good and evil," was an idiom that meant "knowledge of everything." Since, in this story, only God can know everything, Adam and Eve are trying to play God by taking from the fruit.

Even if you don't believe in God, you can probably appreciate the caution against over-reaching.

Discussion

Let's explore that idea a little more. What is the difference between setting ambitious goals for ourselves and over-reaching? When do we humans "play God" to our detriment? Is there anything in Genesis 3 that can help us not fall into the trap of over-reaching?

Also feel free to discuss the fact that people often read all kinds of sexism into this story in Genesis 3 that isn't there. What's that about? Can you think of other examples of stories from the Bible or elsewhere that people have misinterpreted in a way that hurts a group, such as women, people of color, or members of the LGBTQ community?

My Suggested Bottom Line

We should not use Genesis 3 to put down women. Instead, let's focus on what the story teaches us about over-reaching.

Day Five: The Flood

Reading: Genesis 7

Background

M any Christians insist that the story of the flood is historical even though there is ample reason to think otherwise. I am not going to get into that debate. Instead, I just want to concentrate on the story itself. Putting aside questions of historical accuracy, what does this episode teach us about God and humanity?

For starters, it shows God being, frankly, pretty brutal. Sure, God saves Noah and his family and a portion of the animal population, but the overwhelming majority of animals and people end up drowned because of God's anger with human wickedness. God vows never again to destroy all life by flood. God even hangs God's bow in the sky (the rainbow) as a reminder, not to us humans, but to Godself never to send a worldwide flood again. So God shows mercy, but multitudes of animals and humans are still dead.

It puzzles me that we see this story as great for children (Warning: I am about to be a party-pooper.). It's a popular Vacation Bible School topic, for example. Well-meaning adults—I've participated in this—often create a cardboard ark and have the kids pretend to be different animals. Therein lies the appeal: animals. Kids love 'em, and this story has many, although not really, because, except for a few birds, the animals don't really do anything. They are just there. More important, the notion that containing animals makes this story great for kids seems to overlook or downplay the fact that most of the animals in the story, along with most of the people, end up killed by God. There is a strange disconnection between the horror of the story and the way we often present it to kids, which is as a kind of fun tale because it has lots of animals and a big boat and an old man who is generally depicted as looking like Santa. What does it say about the church that we Christians can take a horrific story and package it so that we feel okay with telling it to our children?

I don't know, but I do know that, despite the brutality of the story, there is much here of value. One important theme is second chances. God could have simply destroyed everyone but decides to give humanity and the rest of creation a second chance, a do-over. Granted, it's a do-over involving the deaths of countless souls, but at least there is some sort of second chance. Humans have made a mess, and God responds with a kind of clean up and reboot.

Discussion

What can we learn about starting over, cleaning up, rebooting? I don't think the lesson is that we should kill everyone who is a problem, an idea that is both repulsive and inconsistent with the Bible when taken as a whole. Let's think more metaphorically. When a situation is broken, how can we clean up and start over rather than quit? How do we rebuild? When you lose your job or end up addicted to drugs or in a divorce, you may want to give up on life. Instead, how can you start over?

The flood story suggests that starting over involves identifying the good and working with that. That's what God does. God focuses on Noah and family. Perhaps, in a bad situation, there is always someone or something good that we can work with. As Mr. Rogers's mother said to him regarding crisis, "Look for the helpers." No matter how disastrous a situation is, there is always someone or something we can work with to make things better, just as God works with Noah.

Unfortunately, it won't be long before Noah and descendants start to ruin things, just as their pre-flood ancestors did. And, as we will see, throughout the Bible God gets angry but never gives up.

Whether you believe in God or not, you can see the character of God as a model for not giving up.

My Suggested Bottom Line

The flood story is more gruesome than most of us admit, but it does show God not giving up on humanity and creation. We shouldn't, either.

Day Six: Abraham and Sarah and Children

Reading: Genesis 12:1–4

Background

Note, in Genesis 12, Abraham is called "Abram," but later God will change his name to "Abraham" and will change his wife's name from "Sarai" to "Sarah." Name-changing is a motif in the Bible and often indicates that a person has taken on a new role. "Abraham," for instance, means "father of a multitude," which is what he will become.

Abraham and Sarah are among the most important people in the Bible because it is with them that God's chosen people begin. The Bible, you see, focuses on the nation of Israel and its citizens, the Israelites, who, again, are also called the Hebrews and, later, the Jews. The Jews trace their roots back to Abraham, with whom God establishes a testament or covenant, which is an arrangement or agreement between two parties. In this case, God establishes the covenant, which is that God will make Abraham the father of a great nation and will grant that great nation the Promised Land to live in. Given that Sarah is to be the mother of this nation, the covenant applies to her, as well. In return, Abraham and Sarah and their descendants must worship only God. Remember that, in those days, polytheism (worshipping multiple gods) was the norm, but God is calling Abraham and Sarah and descendants to be monotheists (worshippers of only one god).

The rest of the book of Genesis is about Abraham and Sarah and their descendants, with the focus being on their son Isaac; his sons, Jacob and Esau; and then Jacob's twelve sons, most notably Joseph. Genesis ends with Joseph and family living in Egypt happily ever after, at least until we get to the book of Exodus, which tells of the Egyptians enslaving the Hebrews.

By the way, according to the New Testament, Christians are linked to Abraham and Sarah through Christ, so, in a sense, those two people are the progenitors of Christianity, as well as Judaism. Further, Islam traces its roots back to Abraham, called Ibrahim in the Qur'an. In fact, we scholars often refer to these three religions as the Abrahamic Faiths, or, if you want to sound in-the-know, the Abrahamics.

Discussion

The Bible stresses Abraham's faith. He continues to obey and trust in God. That said, although Abraham is largely devoted to God, he does have moments of faltering faith. Most notable is that he fathers a child with his wife Sarah's handmaid, Hagar, because he is not confident that he will ever have a child by Sarah, even though God promised that he would. Actually, it is Sarah who suggests that Abraham do that, but he does not resist. He does not say, for instance, "No, Sarah. I don't need to have sex with Hagar. We just need to trust God and hang in there." So both Sarah and Abraham demonstrate less-than-perfect faith.

What we see, then, is messiness. Yes, Abraham is faithful, but he falters. His story gives us permission not to be perfect in our commitment to whatever or whoever is important to us, such as nation, family, career, or a cause. We will falter. I try to be a good father and husband and grandfather, but am I always? Of course not. I try to be a dedicated feminist committed to gender equity, but I don't always succeed at that, either. We wobble in our faith and commitment, and we should forgive ourselves and one another for that wobbling.

The story can also simply challenge us to think seriously about what is of the highest importance to us. What matters most to you? Family, probably, but what else? Is there some aspect of yourself, some trait or passion, that you just could not give up? Why is that so important to you? Just as Abraham is devoted to God, what or whom are you devoted to? Could anything or anyone cause you to violate that devotion?

My Suggested Bottom Line

Abraham and Sarah are flawed models of faith whose story stresses the value of, for the most part, not giving up on God.

Day Seven: Joseph

Reading: Genesis 37

Background

T he Joseph saga is fascinating. No wonder Andrew Lloyd Webber made a musical about it. The plot is engaging, the characters are memorable, and the themes are timeless.

For starters, we have a remarkable portrait of a dysfunctional family. Joseph, who is clearly his father's favorite, is telling his already envious brothers that, according to his dreams, someday they will bow before him. No wonder they plot to kill him. Fortunately, they decide on the more humane but still vicious plan of selling him into slavery and then telling their father that Joseph was killed by wild animals.

In Egypt, Joseph is a slave who gets accused falsely of attempted sexual assault by Potiphar's wife, who is simply angry that Joseph won't have sex with her. Joseph is thrown in jail, where he develops a reputation for interpreting dreams correctly. Pharaoh, struggling to make sense of his own dreams, learns of this talented Hebrew, who explains to Pharaoh that his dreams are predicting seven years of plenty for Egypt followed by seven years of severe famine. Therefore, Egypt needs to stock up to prepare for that famine. Pharaoh decides to appoint Joseph to be in charge of that undertaking. Years later, during the famine, guess who shows up looking for food? That's right, Joseph's brothers, who do not recognize him at first. When he meets them, he tests them to see if they have become more honorable men. When he sees that they have, he reveals his identity and invites them and father Jacob to live with him in Egypt.

Discussion

Several themes emerge from this story. One is the danger of envy. The brothers do what they do because they are envious of Joseph. How does envy cause us to engage in toxic, selfish behavior? We also have the dangers of showing favoritism, as Jacob does with Joseph. The story challenges us to examine ourselves for envy and/ or favoritism and to consider how those traits may be polluting our lives and the lives of those around us.

What about this whole business of interpreting dreams? In the ancient world, people often believed that the gods/God communicated to them through dreams. While some of us still believe that today, many of us are more skeptical. We certainly know that, even if we believe that God communicates to us through dreams, any given dream could just as easily be merely an expression of issues buried in our subconscious. Truth be told, we often don't know what's going on with our dreams. So what do we do with them?

Here's a suggestion: we interpret dreams in ways that help us to be better toward others and ourselves. Is that a wise guideline for dream interpretation, regardless of where the dream comes from?

When I was a parish pastor, someone would occasionally share with me a dream she or he had had, often seeking my interpretation. My response tended to be to ask the person how the dream made her feel. For instance, if the dream was about a recently dead loved one, it would generally be a source of comfort for the person. So that's what we'd focus on.

Did the dream come from God? Was the deceased actually communicating with the bereaved through the dream? I don't know. There is no way to know, but we could talk about how the dream made the dreamer feel and go from there.

On May 25, 2019, I had a dream about my biological father, who was abusive and has been dead for thirty-two years. In the dream, he was not the frightening figure he had been in life, and I felt no ill will toward him. Instead, I tried to help him connect with a girl he had liked back in high school. I was trying to assist this man who had hurt me. I woke up thinking that the dream was suggesting that I was ready to move on from the pain he had caused me. I don't know if that dream came from God, but I saw it as leading me in a positive direction.

Can you recall a dream and how it made you feel? What impact did the dream have on you?

Finally, another important theme in the Joseph saga is that we often understand life better in retrospect. Joseph goes through a terrible ordeal but then finds out at the end that God was with him all along, guiding his life toward eventual happiness. Now, I don't know how much of a role God plays in our lives and how that relates to our free will, but I do know that frequently, when we look back on a difficult period, we can see positive forces at work that we couldn't see at the time. Can you think of an example of that happening in your life or the life of someone else?

My Suggested Bottom Line

The Joseph saga is a rich story that can lead to great discussions about how to deal with envy, dreams, and misfortune.

Day Eight: Tamar

Reading: Genesis 38

Background

Here we have the story of Tamar, the daughter-in-law of Judah, one of Jacob's sons and Joseph's brothers. Tamar's husband, who was evil, dies, so now Tamar is a widow and thus at a severe economic and social disadvantage. She also has no children, so she is at an even greater disadvantage. According to Jewish law, her husband's brother is supposed to take care of her, including by impregnating her so that she can have a child, but he refuses and is struck dead. Judah promises her that his other son will step up, but he never makes good on that promise. In response, Tamar disguises herself as a prostitute and tricks Judah into having sex with her so that she can get pregnant. Because he does not have payment at the time, she takes his signet, cord, and staff as collateral. Later, Judah cannot find her. A few months pass, and now Tamar is visibly pregnant. Judah orders her to be put to death because he has heard that she got pregnant by prostitution. She then produces Judah's own signet, cord, and staff as a way of showing that Judah was the one who had impregnated her. As a result, he pardons her. She gives birth to twins.

Discussion

This story is striking for at least two reasons. First, it shows a woman being a victim of a patriarchal society but then succeeding through outwitting at least one of the men of that society, Judah. She becomes a widow because God kills her husband as punishment for his wickedness. Her husband's brother lets her down. Judah also lets her down. She then outsmarts Judah, who was going to have her executed for prostitution even though he is the one who slept with her. Amazing! In this world in which men hold the power, this woman manages to emerge the victor. Perhaps it is for this remarkable achievement that, in Matthew's gospel in the New Testament, Tamar is one of only four women mentioned in Jesus' genealogy.

So then, one question to ask is, "How are women still at a disadvantage today, and what can we do to help them? Specifically, how can we use the male-dominated rules of society against themselves in the name of helping women?" I'm not saying we should break laws, and I am not saying that all men are evil and should be tricked. I am saying that sometimes we need to find clever, creative ways to take a flawed system and use it to advance justice. How can we do that?

The second remarkable feature of this story is where it is located in the book of Genesis. Did you notice? It interrupts the Joseph saga. In Chapter 37, Joseph's jealous brothers have sold him into slavery. In Chapter 39, the story continues. Chapter 38, which tells of Tamar, is unrelated. So why is it there? Maybe it's an editing mistake; we have a few of those in the Bible. But what if it isn't? What if the story of Tamar intentionally interrupts the Joseph saga?

Maybe we are supposed to compare the Tamar story to the Joseph saga, so let's do that. Talk about how this story is similar to and/or different from the Joseph saga. What light does it shed on the longer and more significant Joseph story? What's going on here? What is the writer/editor of this part of Genesis trying to convey?

Readers of the Bible often forget that it is, among other things, a work of literature. As such, it is full of literary devices and other features, including stories within stories. As a literature scholar and fiction writer, I am attentive to the literary nature of the Bible, but sometimes that nature is surprising to readers. We contemporary readers often underestimate the sophistication of ancient writers, but here we have what looks like a pretty crafty literary move: the placement of a seemingly unrelated story in the middle of a larger story. Why?

My Suggested Bottom Line

The story of Tamar shows a woman having power in a man's world, and its placement invites comparison with the Joseph saga.

Day Nine: Moses

Introduction to Exodus and the "Historical" Books

I have "history" and "historical" in quotes because the ancient understanding of the writing of history (historiography) and the modern understanding are different. Today, writing history is all about accuracy (that's what we tell ourselves, anyway). You want to recount the past as accurately as possible. In the ancient world, however, the writing of history was less about accuracy and more about showing how the past events were relevant to the present. So then, ancient historiographers often compromised accuracy for the sake of making a point that would be relevant to their readers.

We experience something similar in movies based on true stories. We readily accept that filmmakers take liberties with actual events. We are savvy enough to know that what we are seeing is not necessarily accurate but is being presented so as to strike a chord with us viewers. For instance, the Nazis did not really chase after the von Trapps, as they do in *The Sound of Music* (1965), but depicting the Nazis as doing that probably struck a profound note with viewers, many of whom could still recall vividly the long nightmare that had been World War II. Accuracy was compromised for relevance.

It is therefore unlikely that every event mentioned in the Bible happened exactly as reported. Now, some of you will be fine with that conclusion, while others of you will squirm. Let me suggest, as I did in the previous section, that, instead of worrying about what actually happened, we focus on the literary and thematic value of the story. Instead of asking, "How did it happen?" let's focus instead on "What does it mean?"

Reading: Exodus 11

Background

With that point aside, let us move on to Moses, one of the most important figures in the Bible. We first meet him in the book of Exodus, the second book of the Bible, which tells one of the Good Book's most significant stories: the Exodus, which is the freeing of the Israelites or Hebrews (later called the Jews) from slavery in Egypt. They were in Egypt in the first place because of what had happened with Joseph, and initially life was good for them. Then a wicked pharaoh took to the throne and enslaved them. By the way, "pharaoh" is not a name but the title for the ruler of Egypt. We don't know which pharaoh was in power at the time of Moses, but many of us scholars think it may have been Ramses II. It doesn't really matter, though; all we need to know is that the pharaoh in power in Exodus oppresses the Israelites.

From the burning bush, God calls Moses to confront Pharaoh to demand that he release God's people from slavery. Pharaoh says no. God sends ten plagues, the last of which is the death of firstborn males in Egypt. Pharaoh finally relents but changes his mind and sends the Egyptian army after the departing Hebrews. God, however, parts the Red Sea (actually the Sea of Reeds; "Red Sea" is a mistranslation) so that the Israelites can escape by walking through the sea. When the Egyptian army follows, the sea closes, killing everyone.

Next, the Israelites spend forty years wandering in the wilderness, where they often complain and disobey God. Eventually, though, God allows them to enter Canaan, the land God promised to them. Moses, however, is not allowed to enter and dies just outside the border (such a gyp for Moses).

I must confess that I find this story disturbing. I get that God rescues thousands of people from slavery; that's wonderful.

It troubles me, though, that many Egyptians have to suffer and die in the process. Even more troubling is that Pharaoh is so stubborn because God makes him so (ex., Exodus 10:1). God hardens Pharaoh's heart. Lives could have been spared if God had just made Pharaoh agree to let the Israelites go in the first place. So why didn't God just do that? Troubling.

I don't know what to make of that part of the plot, but I do know this: Moses and his story illustrate God working through a person to rescue a multitude of people from slavery. We have a story of socio-economic injustice: one group of people enslaving another. This saga tells of the liberation of those enslaved people. It is not surprising that African American slaves connected with this story, seeing it as reflecting their own plight and as offering hope for liberation.

That said, the Bible's attitude toward slavery is mixed. Ephesians 6:5 says, "Slaves, obey your earthly masters with fear and trembling," but Galatians 3:28 says, "[T]here is no longer slave or free" (NRSV). So which is it? I suspect that the answer is probably that slavery was allowed but that the people of God were supposed to be loving and kind to their slaves. It's also important to note that slavery in the biblical world was different from, say, slavery in the United States before the Civil War or modern day slavery, also known as human trafficking. Regardless, slavery is indefensible. In any case, the Bible repeatedly stresses that we are to care for the oppressed and less fortunate, including slaves.

Discussion

Moses is the rescuer of the oppressed. Likewise, we are to do what we can to rescue the oppressed. For instance, what can you do about human trafficking, modern day slavery? What committee can you join or form? What donations of money and talent can you make? The Bible is bumpy, but overall it calls for the freeing of the oppressed. How can you and I help with that? How can we put aside religious and other differences to help free those who are treated so horribly by others? Discuss how you can be a modern day Moses.

Born a slave, Harriet Tubman (ca. 1822–1913) got her freedom and led about thirteen missions to free approximately seventy people from slavery through her use of the Underground Railroad. She also helped abolitionist John Brown recruit men for his raid on Harpers Ferry, and, during the Civil War, she was an armed scout and spy for the Union Army. After the war, she worked to get women the right to vote. Her nickname: Moses.

My Suggested Bottom Line

The story of Moses is ultimately about freeing the enslaved.

Day Ten: Deborah

Reading: Judges 4 and 5

Background

When my students and I discuss how women were treated in antiquity (and, frankly, throughout much of history), we of course talk about how, in the world of the Bible, women had second-class status. However, sometimes my students conclude from that terrible fact that no woman had any rights or authority ever, but that is not true. Women did enjoy some rights and authority, and a few women rose to prominence. Deborah was one of them.

Whether Deborah actually existed or not, we still have a story about a woman of power. She is a judge, a type of military and political ruler prominent in Israel before the establishment of the monarchy. People seek her out for guidance, and she encourages Barak, a military leader, toward victory.

Throughout literature, women of power are often sexualized; that is, their power is portrayed as coming at least in part from their ability to seduce men. Such a portrayal reinforces a long-standing view in our society of women as sex objects. But Deborah is not sexualized. She has power because she is blessed by God with wisdom and military prowess, period.

Adding to this portrait of a powerful woman is a subplot in the Deborah story involving another woman, Jael. When the enemy military leader Sisera falls asleep, Jael sneaks up to him and kills him by driving a tent stake through his head with a hammer. Yikes!

Again, the story does not sexualize Jael, although you could make the case that the tent stake is a kind of phallic symbol. Jael also is a bit of a seductress in that she gives Sisera milk to drink in a successful attempt to lull him to sleep. Even so, she does not use her sexuality to trick him; she uses her wits and physical strength.

Fun fact: Judges 5, which contains the Song of Deborah (a celebratory retelling of Deborah's heroism), is generally considered one of the oldest parts of the Bible.

By the way, Deborah and Jael remind me of Judith, a woman found in non-Protestant versions of the Old Testament who kills the evil Holofernes by beheading him, an event that Baroque painter Artemisia Gentileschi (1593-ca. 1656) depicted in her work.

Discussion

What do you think of Deborah and Jael as heroines? Are there problems with these characters that could hurt how we view women? For instance, does the story of Jael reinforce the stereotype of women being conniving or the sexist saying that "Hell hath no fury like a woman scorned"?

One of the extraordinary features of the Bible is that, to a point, it is self-critical. In this case, for instance, we have the Bible overwhelmingly featuring men in power and indicating that men should indeed have that power. But then, the Bible has moments that go against that idea by showing women in power over men. You will see this self-critical aspect of the Bible repeatedly. The Bible will advance a claim and then propose the opposite of that claim. What do you make of that feature of the Good Book? Is it a strength or weakness? What can learn from it? Can we learn, for instance, the value of questioning our assumptions and critiquing our conclusions?

My Suggested Bottom Line

The story of Deborah (and Jael) shows that even in biblical times women sometimes rose to positions of heroic power.

Day Eleven: Ruth

Reading: The Book of Ruth

Background

S peaking of women in power, here we have an entire book of the Bible devoted to a woman. Granted, it's only four chapters, but it is nevertheless notable that a world that featured and favored male dominance would bother to focus on a woman. Actually, the story focuses on two women, Ruth and her mother-in-law, Naomi, to whom Ruth vows loyalty. The story goes on to tell of how Ruth eventually ends up marrying a man named Boaz and has a child. So then, unlike the story of Deborah, this story features a woman embracing a traditional role, that of wife and mother. Ruth is not a heroine because she is a great warrior or political leader like Deborah; she is a heroine because of her devotion as a family woman.

While I would love to see Ruth be strong in a way that goes against the gender stereotype of woman-as-committed-to-family, I still appreciate that a woman is being celebrated at all. Besides, family is, of course, extremely important. Stories about heroic men often say little about their devotion to family, so it is wonderful to have a tale that shows the value of family. By the way, Boaz, the man of the story, also is depicted as caring about family. He is no warrior or political leader. His heroism lies in his decency toward Ruth.

This quiet tale stands in telling contrast to what surrounds it. The book preceding it, Judges, and the book following it, 1 Samuel, both feature military conquest and political machinations. In fact,

2 Samuel, 1 and 2 Kings, and 1 and 2 Chronicles all do, too. Men engaging in lots and lots of slaughter and politicking dominate those books. How refreshing to have the little book of Ruth offering a non-violent, not-epic but still important story of good people being decent toward each other. The tale is valuable in part because of this gentler contrast it provides, and in part because of its focus on women. In addition, the story connects to what follows because Ruth, we are told at the end, turns out to be the great-grandmother of Israel's most revered king, David, who is featured later.

Finally, it is noteworthy that Ruth is a foreigner. She is from Moab. She comes to Israel as an immigrant. Thus, we have an outsider being held up as a heroine and influencing the royal line of the great King David.

Discussion

This story highlights the importance of loyalty. Ruth pledges deathless devotion to her mother-in-law. Whom are you loyal to? How far are you willing to go for your loyalty? Ruth goes so far as to move to another country and convert to Naomi's religion, Judaism. How far would you be willing to go as a show of loyalty? Would you move to another country and change your religion? Would you change your political party? Where is the limit for you?

As I said, the book of Ruth features an outsider, a foreigner. The Bible has a mixed attitude toward outsiders, but it basically welcomes them as long as they do not pose a threat to the culture and religion of the people of Israel. In the Gospels, actually, Jesus is even more open to outsiders, repeatedly making a point of welcoming them. Further, all throughout the Bible, hospitality is emphasized.

Whom do we consider to be outsiders? How do we treat them? How can we show them hospitality? What excuses do we make for not showing them hospitality?

Finally, the book of Ruth's emphasis on women and family is instructive. There has long been a tendency to think of heroism in terms of men winning battles and doing other such grand acts, but

Ruth offers a different kind of heroism. Who are the unsung heroes and heroines in our society? For that matter, what is a hero? Who are the heroes and heroines who help to make our societies safer and our families stronger? How can Ruth and Boaz be models of heroism for you and me?

The difference between the book of Ruth and the historical books that surround it is similar to the difference between the Greek poets Sappho of Lesbos (d. 580 BCE) and Homer (8th or 7th century BCE). Homer's wrote epics, long narratives of military men fighting battles. Sappho wrote lyric poetry, short works about relationships, most notably between women (the word "lesbian" comes from her island of origin). One writer tells "large" stories of men fighting, while the other tells "smaller" stories of relationships and love. We need both models of heroism.

By the way, one of my passions is romance/women's fiction. I have an MFA in Writing Popular Fiction for which I specialized in romance/women's fiction and trying to write it. Romance/women's fiction sometimes tells of women being warriors but often celebrates the everyday lives of women dealing with loved ones (among other things, such as careers). Sometimes this kind of story gets snobbishly dismissed as "chick lit," but the book of Ruth suggests that we should take these tales more seriously. After all, really, there are few things more important than relationships.

My Suggested Bottom Line

The book of Ruth offers a stunning contrast to the bloodier stories that surround it by focusing on a foreign woman's acts of heroic decency toward her mother-in-law and Boaz, the man she ends up marrying.

Day Twelve: David and Goliath

Reading: 1 Samuel 17

Background

The concept of young David going up against the gigantic, well-armored warrior, Goliath, and winning has become archetypal even among people who have never read the Bible. Of course, David is able to beat the odds and kill the giant because God is on his side, but the story is often secularized into being about killing giants in other ways.

An intriguing example of this God-free way of thinking about the David and Goliath story is found in Malcolm Gladwell's engaging 2013 book, *David and Goliath*, in which Gladwell argues that what often appears to be a strength can actually be a weakness that brings about an upset. In the case of our biblical story, which opens Gladwell's book, the author speculates convincingly that this giant, Goliath, may have actually had some physical afflictions as a result of his huge size that made him an easy target. For instance, Gladwell contends that some people of exceptional height have as a side effect bad eyesight and trouble moving. So then, while Goliath looked invincible, he was actually quite vulnerable. David was victorious in part because of Goliath's stature, not in spite of it.[1]

Gladwell's conclusions raise some questions for me—I wonder, for instance, why he assumes that the biblical account is historically accurate when ancient historical narratives are notoriously

---

1. Gladwell, *David and Goliath*, 3–15.

unreliable—but his basic point still holds: sometimes what appears to be an advantage actually can be a liability. We have certainly seen that dynamic with empires or even large corporations. They become so huge that they can no longer function properly and thus fall apart.

Although I find Gladwell's ideas illuminating, I want to go back to the role that God plays in the David and Goliath story. David's success is due to God's intervention, at least according to 1 Samuel 17. David says as much in a speech he makes right before killing Goliath (vv. 45–47). So then, this story is about God's strength more than it is about David's cleverness or Goliath's bad eyesight.

Discussion

One relevant discussion topic, then, is the application of Gladwell's idea that the apparent strength of an opponent could actually be a weakness that we can use against that opponent. Another topic is how to stay focused on something greater than ourselves, such as Truth or Love, in a way that enables us to fell Goliaths.

As we think about how to face Goliaths, it makes sense to ask who our Goliaths are. Just because something is large and powerful doesn't mean it's bad, and just because someone is smaller and appears to be weaker doesn't mean that she or he is on the side of right. Think and talk about this. Who are the Goliaths of our society? What makes them so? Why should they be stopped?

You can think about your personal life, too. Who are the Goliaths in your life? How can you stop them? How can strengths and weaknesses and something greater than yourself, such as Love, help you be successful?

In 2014, when she was about twenty-one, Iraqi Nadia Murad was kidnapped by the Islamic State. For three months, she was a sex slave, sold from man to man like property, repeatedly raped, beaten, and tortured. She was targeted in no small part because she was a member of the oft-persecuted Yazidi ethno-religious minority. Finally, in part through the help of a sympathetic family, she managed to escape. She has been working with the United Nations to bring justice for the Yazidi and other victims. In 2018, Murad won the Nobel Peace Prize. She has truly been a David fighting against the Goliaths of the Islamic State and human trafficking.

Given the overarching themes of the Bible, I'd have to say that the Goliaths are those forces that interfere with love, peace, and living out one's calling. What are those in your life? How can you defeat them?

One mistake we sometimes make, however, is we see anyone who is different as a Goliath. Often we find great strength and unity in getting to know better people different from ourselves. Frequently, the real Goliath is our prejudice.

Another common Goliath is addiction. A few years ago, a dear friend of mine ended up basically failing college and getting arrested because of a marijuana addiction that led to dealing. I was there when he was taken away in handcuffs. He had a huge Goliath, drug addiction, that led to months of hearings, a suspension of his license, thousands of dollars in fees and fines, and, worst of all, humiliation. He went to rehab and AA/NA (he went back and forth between the two since he also had a drinking problem). He started his life over. He worked for years in a job he hated so that he could pay off fees and reboot his life. Occasionally he would relapse. Today, his life is not perfect, of course, but he is clean and sober, working a job he likes, and doing well in school. How did he do it? Prayer, meetings, family, friends, determination.

The Goliath did not fall suddenly or dramatically, but it fell.

What is your Goliath? How will you conquer it?

My Suggested Bottom Line

The story of David and Goliath continues to challenge us with how to turn strengths into weaknesses and to trust in something greater than ourselves, such as God, Truth, or Love.

Day Thirteen: David and Bathsheba

Reading: 2 Samuel 11

Background

Overall, David's reputation is sterling, although he is portrayed more positively in 1 and 2 Chronicles than in 1 and 2 Samuel. David is the ultimate king. He is handsome, a skillful warrior, a brilliant musician, and, most important, devoted to God. In fact, it is prophesied that the Messiah (the Bible's term for a special chosen hero) will be a descendent of David; sure enough, Jesus is just such a descendent.

Nevertheless, even David has his sins, the most notorious of which is his affair with Bathsheba, the wife of Uriah the Hittite. In fact, not only does he have sex with her—by the way, it is unclear whether Bathsheba wants to have sex with him—and thus commits at least adultery, a crime punishable by death, but he gets her pregnant. When her husband, Uriah, returns home from battle, David tries to get him to sleep with Bathsheba so that he will think the child is his. But Uriah does not want to have sexual relations with his wife because he is in the midst of a military campaign and so is abstaining as a kind of discipline and code of honor. David then arranges for Uriah to be positioned in the front lines and for other soldiers to fall back, thereby increasing the likelihood of Uriah being killed in battle, which happens. So David is guilty of adultery and then, indirectly, murder to protect himself from the consequences of his adultery.

But David has not gotten away with this, for the prophet Nathan, to whom God has revealed the truth, confronts David. Now, confronting the king with an accusation could get a person executed, so Nathan slyly tricks David into condemning himself by asking David how he would rule in a hypothetical scenario in which a wealthy man takes a ewe from a poor man who has nothing else. When David declares that such a person should be put to death, Nathan replies, "You are that man!" David repents. God punishes him by killing the baby that Bathsheba is pregnant with (a punishment that strikes me as unfair toward both Bathsheba and, even more, the baby). However, God forgives him and allows him to remain on the throne. In fact, David and Bathsheba have another child, Solomon, who will be the next king.

Fun fact: As I mentioned a few days ago, in the Gospel of Matthew, we find a genealogy of Jesus' ancestors. Only four women are mentioned (not counting Mary). One of them is Bathsheba, although she is not referred to by name but as "the wife of Uriah the Hittite."

Discussion

One valuable discussion topic would be the flawed nature of our heroes. Even people we admire the most have their sins. The Bible is not saying that we should ignore those sins; David is punished for his. But this story does imply that we perhaps need to remember that our great heroes and heroines might do terrible things, and we should do our best to forgive them.

That said, though, another valuable discussion topic is the victimization of Bathsheba. Here is a woman who had done nothing wrong. She was simply bathing on the roof when the king decided he wanted to have sex with her. Talk about a misuse of power! I imagine that one probably did not think that saying no to the king was a safe option. It is telling, by the way, that Bathsheba says virtually nothing through this entire story; she has virtually no voice. To make matters worse, David arranges for Bathsheba's husband to be killed. Of course that fate is horrible for the husband, but it is also horrible for Bathsheba. In the 1951 film, *David and Bathsheba*, Bathsheba is more of a willing participant in the love affair, but she is passive in the biblical account.

Could it be that this story is, among other things, an illustration of how sometimes women are used as pawns by men?

This is also a story about class and power, isn't it? David is able to have sex with Bathsheba and kill her husband because of his power as king. As Nathan reveals in his indicting story, David is wealthy while Uriah is much poorer, and David takes that poorer man's wife. Ancient Israel allowed its kings to have a harem, but David takes Uriah's sole spouse.

On the whole, the Bible denounces the exploitation of the poor and other marginalized people, and the Bible denounces people in power using that power for selfish gain. Discuss contemporary examples of such exploitation today. How can you or I be a Nathan in response to such injustice? How are we in danger of being David?

Yes, David is forgiven, but his story still warns against the oppression of women and people of lower socio-economic classes.

My Suggested Bottom Line

The story of David and Bathsheba shows that even our greatest heroes and heroines are flawed and also warns against the oppression of the marginalized, in this case women and people of lower income.

Day Fourteen: Solomon

Reading: 1 Kings 3

Background

Solomon, the son of David and Bathsheba, succeeds his father as king of Israel. His greatest achievement is the building of the Temple, the holiest place on Earth for the Israelites. That Temple, which was located in Israel's capital city of Jerusalem, would be destroyed by the Babylonians in 587/6 BCE (it is unclear whether the event happened in 587 of 586) and then rebuilt only to be destroyed again by the Romans in 70 CE. A portion of the complex, the Western Wall, still stands today.

Solomon's most famous attribute is his wisdom. In the reading I selected, God offers Solomon anything, and Solomon responds by requesting, not wealth or honor, but wisdom, a request that so pleases God that he gives Solomon wealth and honor, as well. Then we see a demonstration of that wisdom when Solomon resolves the rather troubling situation between two women fighting over a baby. He offers the horrific solution of slicing the baby in two and giving half to each mother, knowing that the real mother would never consent to such a plan and so would protest. Sure enough, one of the women says that she would rather the other woman receive the baby than for it to be cut in half, while the second woman is fine with Solomon's proposal. He then presents the baby to the first woman, knowing that she must be the real mother.

Solomon goes on to be, on the whole, a great king, but, like his father, he has his sins, most notably his rejection of God in favor of other gods. You see, Solomon has many wives (700, along with 300 concubines). Now, in the world of the Old Testament, having many wives was not in of itself considered immoral. Polygamy was permissible in ancient Israel (for men, not for women), and kings often married foreign women as a way of forming a treaty or alliance with that foreign power. While this practice is profoundly disturbing for us in the twenty-first century, in the biblical world it is not an issue. The problem, according to the Bible, is that Solomon allows his wives to worship these other gods and thus pulls away from God, who throughout the Bible insists on monotheism.

The biblical books of Proverbs, Ecclesiastes, and Song of Solomon are often attributed to Solomon and are seen as illustrative of his great wisdom. However, most of us scholars contend that Solomon probably did not actually write these books because they have features suggesting a later composition date. Think what you wish. We will look at those books later. In any case, that these works are attributed to Solomon reflects his legacy of great wisdom.

Discussion

One germane topic for discussion is the importance of wisdom. Solomon is wise enough not to ask for wealth and honor but for this special attribute. The Bible repeatedly stresses the importance of wisdom over wealth, power, and fame. We will look closer at the Bible's understanding of this trait in a few days, but for now why not discuss what you think wisdom is and how our society both supports and undercuts it? What is the difference between being wise and being smart? Does wisdom come with age? How can we cultivate wisdom? How can we teach it in school?

A second relevant topic is Solomon losing sight of God. It would be wrong to blame his many wives for distracting him. Solomon alone is responsible for his actions. What leads us astray from our focus? Solomon's tremendous wealth and power seem to contribute to his downfall. How can we protect ourselves from downfalls when we achieve success?

My Suggested Bottom Line

The story of Solomon celebrates wisdom and warns against losing sight of what really matters.

Day Fifteen: Esther

Reading: Esther 7

Background

Before getting into the book of Esther, I need to provide some historical background so that you understand Esther's context.

After Solomon's death, Israel split into two kingdoms: the Northern Kingdom, called Israel, and the Southern Kingdom, called Judah (just like the person's name we encountered earlier). David's descendants continued to rule in the Southern Kingdom, in Jerusalem, while the Northern Kingdom had a separate line of kings. In 722/1 BCE, the Assyrian Empire (technically the Neo-Assyrian Empire) attacked and destroyed the Northern Kingdom. In 587/6 BCE, the Babylonian Empire (technically the Neo-Babylonian Empire) attacked Judah, destroyed Jerusalem and the Temple, and took a large portion of the population into captivity. That captivity is known as the Exile and is one of the most important events in the Old Testament. It ended in 538 BCE, when King Cyrus of Persia, who defeated the Babylonians, liberated the people of Judah to return home to rebuild, although some Jews remained in foreign lands. The book of Esther tells of Jews living in Persia and is set sometime around the late 400s BCE, although many of us scholars think this book is a work of fiction.

The book of Esther never mentions God. Not once. This reads like a secular story. In fact, Esther is one of only two biblical books never to mention God. So why is this book in the Bible? Well, the book of Esther is obviously about the Jews, God's chosen people, and seems to imply God's guidance. We are likely supposed to conclude that Esther is successful because God is with her.

The story is chilling. Set in Persia, the book tells of Esther, who is secretly Jewish, becoming the queen and then working to prevent a genocide against her people that the evil Haman wishes to carry out as revenge against Mordecai, Esther's cousin and guardian, because of his refusal to bow to Haman (since such an act would be idolatrous). Haman is so enraged by Mordecai's refusal to bow before him that Haman decides that Mordecai and every other Jew in Persia should be killed. Esther curries the favor of her husband the king by holding two dinners for him. She then reveals that she is Jewish herself and begs the king to stop Haman's horrible plan. Although the king cannot legally reverse the decree for genocide, he can decree that all Jews be armed so that they can protect themselves. They end up slaughtering their attackers, and Haman is hanged from the very gallows he had erected for Mordecai. The story, by the way, is the basis for the Jewish festival of Purim, which is held in late winter.

Oh, I said that Esther is one of only two books in the Bible not to mention God. Do you know what the other one is?

Discussion

This is a rather gruesome book full of vengeance. Haman wants to get revenge against Mordecai for not bowing to him, but then Esther and Mordecai get revenge against Haman for his horrible plot. The Bible contains quite a few violent, vicious stories, but it also emphasizes mercy and peace. In fact, overall, the message of mercy and peace prevails.

What do we do, then, with a book like Esther? One positive message is that this book tells of a woman saving the day. Again, in a society that overwhelmingly focused on and favored men, it is especially exciting to see this story of a brave, intelligent woman saving many lives.

Another positive message in the book is its denunciation of a genocide and its demand for justice in the face of evil. The story challenges us to think about how we can use our own abilities and resources to save others.

Along these lines, it is hard to read this story and not think of the Holocaust. How did people step up to save lives during that nightmare of human history? What genocide is happening today, and what are we doing to stop it? It is easy to be complacent and to think that there is nothing you and I can do, but imagine if all people throughout Europe had thought the same during the Holocaust. Esther urges us not to look the other way when evil rises.

In 1994, many members of the Hutu tribe launched a genocide against members of the Tutsi tribe in the small African country of Rwanda. In about one hundred days, approximately a million people, largely Tutsi and moderate Hutu, were killed while most of the rest of the world, including the United States, made excuses not to get involved. Hotel manager Paul Rusesabagina, a Hutu, used his hotel and connections to save the lives of over 1200 people. The movie *Hotel Rwanda* (2004) depicts Rusesabagina's heroism. Like Esther, when evil appeared, he did not look away.

My Suggested Bottom Line

The book of Esther tells of how a woman uses her wits to save the Jews from genocide and so challenges us to go and do likewise.

Day Sixteen: Elijah

Introduction to the Prophets

B efore we turn to Elijah, let's be clear about what a prophet is. A prophet is not a fortuneteller. Sometimes biblical prophets deal with the future (usually the immediate future), sometimes they don't, but their main job is to serve as a special messenger between God and the people. Prophets generally declare a countercultural message, one that goes against the prevailing view of society. Frequently, prophets criticize the people for bad behavior and urge them to change or else face severe consequences. However, prophets also proclaim messages of hope for the people during times of darkness. In addition, prophets often advised the king to keep him on the right track regarding serving God. Oh, and prophets weren't necessarily male.

In the Bible, prophecy fades with the monarchy, but we still have people today who at least function like a prophet. The obvious example is Martin Luther King, a religious figure who declared a countercultural message and offered both a warning and a vision of hope for the future. And, as is often the case with prophets, King was killed for his prophetic work.

Preaching scholar and activist Leah Schade has written an intriguing book on prophetic preaching called *Preaching in the Purple Zone: Ministry in the Red-Blue Divide*, in which she suggests that sermons need to be more prophetic in terms of speaking toward justice issues. However, she notes that such issues are often polarizing. Her solution is that pastors prepare sermons through having deliberative discussions with parishioners. Through this process, people who disagree with one another can learn truly to listen to each other, and the pastor then can preach prophetically in a way that her or his parishioners will be more receptive to. Schade's strategy of deliberative dialogue married to addressing justice issues can be useful for all of us, even those who are not religious.[1]

One can be prophetic even if not a believer in God.

Reading: 1 Kings 18–19

Background

Now that you know what a prophet is, let's move on to Elijah, one of Israel's greatest prophets, the standard against which others would be measured. He is best known for standing up to King Ahab and his wife, Jezebel, who had abandoned worship of God to worship a rival deity, Ba'al.

In these chapters, we have two famous stories about Elijah. First, we have the contest between Ba'al and God, with God as the easy victor. Second, we have Elijah fleeing for his life and hiding on Mount Horeb (also called Mount Sinai), which is the mountain on which Moses received the Ten Commandments hundreds of years earlier. There, Elijah, clearly depressed, declares that he is all alone and that his life is in danger. He then experiences a wind, earthquake, and fire, all ways that God traditionally appears to people in the Bible, but God is not found in any of that. Finally, Elijah hears what is often translated as a "still, small voice."

Many people argue that God is present in the still, small voice and that the point is that God often comes to us in tiny, quiet ways rather than in big, loud ways, but I'm not so sure. There is nothing in the story that indicates that God is present in the still, small voice. In addition, that phrase could also be translated as "the sound of sheer silence." Maybe this quiet moment is simply the calm after the storms. In any case, whether God is present in

---

1. Schade, *Preaching in the Purple Zone*.

the quiet or not, it is clear that Elijah has not been impacted because he says, word for word, what he said before the still, small voice. Verbatim he declares again that he is alone and that his life is in danger. So if God was present in the still, small voice, that point was lost on Elijah.

The story ends with God promising to send Elijah help. So he is not alone after all; God is with him and is sending reinforcements.

One of the points of this passage is that Elijah is not truly alone and hope is not lost, even though he feels alone and hopeless. And God certainly can come to us through a still, small voice. I am just not convinced that, in this case, God is present in the still, small voice (or whatever it is) and that, if he is, Elijah benefits from that presence.

There are other stories about Elijah beyond what I discuss here. Also, there is a prophecy that Elijah will appear before the Messiah comes. In the New Testament, John the Baptist is seen by some as Elijah returned. Also, when Jesus is transfigured on a mountain, two great people from the Old Testament appear with him: Moses and Elijah. And, in Judaism, there are several traditions involving Elijah.

Discussion

One topic for discussion that arises from Chapter 19 is the nature of depression. Elijah feels hopeless. He sees himself as all alone and his future as bleak. In reality, though, he is far from alone, as God tells him, and he is not to be killed by Jezebel. Depression often causes us to have a distorted view of our situation. We see things as far worse than they are.

I have struggled with depression my whole adult life. It's not a severe struggle, but it's there nonetheless. Thanks to medication, therapy, meditation, and maturation, most days I have my depression under control, and when I get depressed, I know how to deal with it constructively. But sometimes, usually in the evening, I cannot shake free from it. I descend into hopelessness. "I'm stupid. I'm a failure. I will never amount to anything. I could die tomorrow, and no one would care." Now, I know on some level that what I am saying and thinking is irrational, but I don't care. At the moment, it feels true, so it is. At that point, the best thing for me to do is to go to bed; a good night's sleep is great for exorcising that demon from me.

How about you? Do you struggle with depression or its sibling, anxiety? You probably know of at least three people who do. What does this passage from 1 Kings teach us about depression and how to treat it?

The Bible is in no way a psychology book and cannot serve as a substitute for, say, talk therapy or medication, but it does show us examples of depressed people and offers suggestions for coping strategies. The Bible encourages us to find, as Jesus says in John 10:10, life abundantly. We will have hardship, but repeatedly the Bible calls us toward, yes sacrifice and suffering, but ultimately joy.

My Suggested Bottom Line

Elijah is one of the great prophets who finds hope amid despair.

Day Seventeen: Isaiah's Call and God's Wrath

Reading: Isaiah 6

Background

Isaiah, Jeremiah, Ezekiel, and Daniel are often collectively known as the "Major Prophets" because the books that bear their names are long. By contrast are the twelve "Minor Prophets," whose books are a good bit shorter. The book of Isaiah is lengthy, sixty-six chapters, and quoted often by the New Testament in reference to Jesus.

The chapter for today is among the most famous of the book of Isaiah. It features what people often consider to be Isaiah's call. He is in the Temple where he has a vision of God's overwhelming grandeur. God is so big that the hem of his robe fills the Temple. Understandably, Isaiah feels unworthy. In fact, he fears for his life, since there was a belief that seeing God meant death for a mortal. Isaiah laments that he has "unclean lips." Then a seraph, a fiery type of angel, removes a burning coal from the altar with a pair of tongs and touches it to Isaiah's lips as a way of cleansing him of his sins. Afterwards, God asks for someone to go and speak, and Isaiah volunteers.

He probably has second thoughts once he hears what he is to say, or not say. God basically orders Isaiah to make sure that the people of Israel do *not* understand the message so that they do not see their error and repent. You see, if they repent, then God will have to show them mercy, and God doesn't want to do that. God wants to assault them with relentless wrath, leaving behind the smallest of remnants.

What a chilling message. God is so angry with the people of Israel that he does not want them to repent. Isaiah's job is to speak so that they do not understand. He will succeed only if he fails.

Why is God so angry with the Israelites? Mainly because they have rejected God and exploited the poor. Later in the book of Isaiah, especially starting with Chapter 40, God shows great mercy to the people of Israel. But first: wrath.

How do we in the twenty-first century deal with God's wrath? Having been raised and trained to focus on God's mercy, I find that wrath makes me uncomfortable. Part of my problem is when people attribute horrible events to God's wrath, such as when Jerry Falwell said 9–11 was God punishing the US because of, among other groups, feminists, gays, and lesbians. Or when one of my nonagenarian parishioners thought that her increasing health problems were a punishment from God and not simply the result of being really old. The Bible does speak of God's wrath, yes, but it is toxic for us to assume that painful events are expressions of that wrath.

Besides, overall, the Bible stresses, not wrath, but mercy. God's anger is brief, but God's mercy is enduring (Psalm 30:5 NRSV). Jesus is certainly far more merciful than wrathful, except, of course, for his threat of eternal damnation for those who do not believe in him. In general, the focus is on mercy. Nevertheless, the wrath still burns in the Bible, so how do we respond to it?

One way is to focus on why God is wrathful. The wrath is often about social injustice. Again, God grows furious over the oppression of the poor. As Catholic social teaching has repeatedly expressed, God has a "preferential option for the poor." We see this message consistently throughout the Bible, including among the prophets. In Isaiah 1, for example, we hear God urge the people to "cease to be evil, / learn to do good; /seek justice, / rescue the oppressed, / defend the orphan, / plead for the widow" (v. 17 NRSV). Caring for the widow and the orphan is a recurring idea in the Bible, with those two people representative of the poor and oppressed in general.

Discussion

Given all the wrath, we could say that sometimes we need to get angry in our efforts to stand up for social justice. How do we do that? How do we make constructive use of our own personal or collective wrath to move society to take better care of widows and orphans? Based on the Bible's overall focus on peace and mercy, it does not make sense for us to behave violently in the name of helping the poor, especially because, when violence breaks out, it is often the poor who suffer the most. So how do we channel our wrath toward advocating for social justice, such as helping the poor?

Another relevant discussion topic has to do with call. God calls Isaiah. What is your calling, if anything? Does everyone have a call? Initially, Isaiah sees himself as sinful, but then the seraph cleanses him. Often in call stories the one being called expresses reluctance about answering in the affirmative. How about you? Are you being called to something that overwhelms you, that you don't feel up to, that you feel unworthy of? What can cleanse you or otherwise help you to take up your call?

If you are searching for a call, what or who can help you find clarity?

Or maybe we don't really have a call that comes from outside us. Maybe we just need to call ourselves to something. What do you think?

My Suggested Bottom Line

The book of Isaiah challenges us to think about our call as well as about how to advocate for social justice.

Day Eighteen: Isaiah and the Suffering Servant

Reading: Isaiah 52:13—53:12

Background

We scholars generally divide the book of Isaiah into three sections. Chapters 1–39 are known as First Isaiah. Chapters 40–55 are known as Second Isaiah. Chapters 56–66 are known as Ethel. Just kidding. Of course, they are known as Third Isaiah. Most of us scholars believe that these sections were likely written by different people at different times in Israel's history (Fun fact: the name Isaiah is never used again in the book after Chapter 39.).

Especially significant is the Exile, which happened in 587/6 BCE and which I covered earlier. Actually, the Exile happened in phases over several years, but 587/6 was especially important because it was in that year that the Babylonians, who had been repeatedly attacking Judah (southern Israel), destroyed the Temple and Jerusalem, killed many Jews and took a portion of the population into exile in Babylon, where they remained until they were liberated by the Persians in 538 BCE.

What does it have to do with Isaiah? We scholars generally think that First Isaiah was written before the Exile, Second Isaiah during, and Third Isaiah after.

Chapter 53, your reading for today, is part of Second Isaiah, when the Jews were in exile and their beloved temple lay in ruins back home, so it is not surprising that it is about suffering. It's not just about any suffering, however, because the one afflicted in the passage is a servant suffering innocently on behalf of others. This idea challenges a recurring view in the Bible: suffering is due to punishment. You suffer because you sinned. We see this idea repeatedly, for example, in Deuteronomy, in which Moses expresses that the people of Israel will be punished for disobeying God and rewarded for obeying him. But Isaiah 53 is one of many passages in the Bible that critiques that simplistic cause-and-effect relationship between conduct and fortune. Here, the suffering is happening to someone who is innocent, not someone who has sinned.

Isaiah 52:13—53:12 is one of four passages in Second Isaiah that we scholars have labeled "Suffering Servant" passages, the other three being 42:1–4, 49:1–6, and 50:4–9. All of these stress this concept of someone suffering, not as punishment, but on behalf of someone else.

Not surprisingly, when Christians hear these passages, especially the more extensive and detailed Isaiah 53, they think "Jesus." In fact, in some churches, Isaiah 53 is read on Good Friday. After all, at the heart of Jesus' identity was that he was morally perfect, innocent, and suffered like a sacrificial lamb for the sake of sinful humanity. "[B]y his bruises we are healed" it says in Isaiah 53:5b, and that idea aligns with the concept of Jesus as God dying on the cross to save humanity. Jesus takes on the punishment for sin so that we don't have to.

Of course, if you are Jewish, then you don't believe that Jesus is the Messiah, let alone God incarnate, so then you would interpret the Suffering Servant passages differently. If the Suffering Servant isn't Jesus, then who is she or he? One possibility is that it is Israel itself, the Jews themselves, who have a long history of being persecuted by other nations. Given that the Suffering Servant passages addressed Jews during the Exile, it is reasonable to conclude that the passages are meant to provide comfort to suffering people. Perhaps the point of Isaiah 53 and other texts is "Don't worry. I haven't forgotten you, and your suffering is not in vain."

We humans don't want our suffering to be in vain, do we? One statement I often hear people make to each other is "Everything happens for a reason" (a statement I have a lot of trouble with, by the way, in part because, if used carelessly, it can make light of suffering), which people generally say to one another, not during good times, but in the face of suffering. The point of uttering the statement is usually to reassure someone that her or his suffering is not purposeless. There is a larger plan, and the misery you experience is a step in that plan. In any case, the point is that we humans tend to be uncomfortable with pointlessness. If we are going to suffer, we want to know why. Perhaps the Suffering Servant passages are grappling with that same issue.

Now, elsewhere in the Bible (such as in Lamentations 1:8) the Jews are told that the Exile happened as a punishment, but here, the focus is on the suffering of the innocent. So then, in the Bible sometimes God's people suffer because they have done wrong, and other times they suffer for the sake of a greater good, as in the case of Isaiah 53.

Discussion

Why there is suffering if God is good enough to want to stop it and powerful enough to stop it is one of the great questions of humanity. The technical term for trying to explain why there is both suffering and an all-loving, all-powerful God is "theodicy." Theodicy is addressed a good bit in the Bible, so we will revisit this crucial topic. For now, focus on Isaiah 53 and theodicy. Why is there suffering in the world? Is all suffering the same? What do you think of the idea of someone suffering on behalf of others? Can you think of examples of such suffering? When should we put up with suffering, and when should we try to break free from it? How do we determine if suffering is worthwhile? Does the prevalence of suffering make it hard to believe in a deity?

Before you discuss this topic, let me stress an important point. If someone is abusing you, you should not just resign yourself to that and put up with the suffering. The Bible does not call us to allow ourselves to be abused. We may sometimes have to endure suffering for the sake of a greater good, but we are never to endure suffering that enables evil.

My Suggested Bottom Line

Isaiah 52:13—53:12 suggests that there may be a benefit to suffering for the sake of someone else. But we never want to justify abuse. People should never tolerate being abused.

Day Nineteen: Amos

Reading: Amos 5:18–24, 7:7–17

Background

As I said, around 930 BCE, Israel split into two kingdoms, the Northern Kingdom, also called "Israel," and the smaller Southern Kingdom, called "Judah."

Amos was from Judah but preached in Israel. He lived during the eighth century at a time when Israel was enjoying military and economic power and stability. Life was good, at least on the surface. The privileged were eating well and attending worship, but their worship was shallow and insincere, and the poor were being neglected. Amos spoke vehemently against that hypocrisy, so much so that he was ordered to leave Israel and return to Judah. Indeed, almost all of the book of Amos blazes with anger against socio-economic injustice and disingenuous worship.

Chapter 5 verses 21–24 illustrate well much of the book's outrage. God says, "I hate, I despise your festivals" (v. 21 NRSV). God declares that he will not accept the people's burnt offerings or listen to their music offered as part of worship. Instead, God commands, "But let justice roll down like / waters, / and righteousness like an / ever-flowing stream" (v. 24 NRSV). The point of these verses is not that people should stop attending worship; after all, the Bible makes clear that worship is essential for the believer. No, the point is that the worship is displeasing to God because justice and righteousness are not being properly carried out.

What Amos railed against 2700 years ago still infuriates many of us today, and that is hypocrisy. We have all experienced hypocrisy; maybe we've been hypocrites ourselves. Someone shows up for worship and is all friendly and devout, maybe even sings in the choir, but then goes home and beats his children. Frederick Douglass (1818–1895), the famous runaway slave and abolitionist, asserts in his 1845 autobiography that the cruelest slave owners were the church-going Christians, and he differentiated between true Christianity and the hypocritical Christianity he often witnessed in America.

Of course, hypocrisy is not just a Christian problem or a religious problem, but a human problem. We're all hypocrites. Sooner or later, every single one of us is a hypocrite because we humans frequently hold high ideals that we simply cannot consistently live up to. Falling short is inevitable, regardless of a person's religious views (including atheism). Nevertheless, hypocrisy is certainly an issue for Jews and Christians. Followers of both religions can see themselves in Amos.

Discussion

What is the cure for hypocrisy? Regardless of whether you are a Jew, Christian, agnostic, or atheist, what can help you reduce your hypocrisy? Perhaps you have indeed found a way to be more consistent in living out your ideals. If so, share that way with others.

Another topic is, once again, social justice. Martin Luther King uses Amos 5:24 in his "I Have a Dream" speech: "We cannot be satisfied so long as the Negro in Mississippi cannot vote and the Negro in New York believes he has nothing for which to vote. No, no, we are not satisfied and will not be satisfied until justice rolls down like waters and righteousness like a mighty stream."[1]

King is obviously talking about racial oppression, even though the book of Amos does not address that issue. The book does address socio-economic oppression, though, and, for King's

1. Martin Luther King, "I Have a Dream."

world (and ours), that oppression has a racial component. So then, his reference to Amos 5:24 is appropriate.

What about for us today? What other socio-economic oppression do we have today? What can we do so that justice rolls down like waters and righteousness like a mighty stream?

A final point to consider from Amos is that he is addressing problems at a time when, for the privileged at least, things appeared to be going well. Amos reminds us that, if others are struggling, then there is work to be done. Just because things are going well for me does not mean they are going well in general. It didn't matter that Israel had a lot of land, military stability, and wealth. There was injustice, so all was far from well.

In fact, about thirty years after Amos's time preaching, Israel (the Northern Kingdom) was destroyed by the Assyrian Empire, so that only Judah, the Southern Kingdom, was left.

What today gives us Americans a false sense of security? What problems are we ignoring? How do we measure prosperity, and how does that measurement lead us to neglect those in deep need?

Amos doesn't mean for us to be paranoid. Nations do go through periods of genuine prosperity. But Amos warns us against being complacent or deceiving ourselves.

My Suggested Bottom Line

Amos challenges us to look at hypocrisy and the problems that lie underneath apparent prosperity.

Day Twenty: Hosea

Reading: Hosea 1

Background

Hosea was from Israel (the Northern Kingdom) and preached there shortly after the time of Amos, when things were starting to fall apart. Especially troubling was Israel's ongoing struggle against the Assyrians, who would eventually destroy Israel, leaving only Judah (the Southern Kingdom) behind.

The most famous, or infamous, feature of the book of Hosea is the first three chapters, which tell the story of Hosea's highly dysfunctional marriage to Gomer. Chapter 1 verse 2 tells us that God orders Hosea to marry a woman who he knows will be unfaithful to him. He does, and sure enough, she is unfaithful. Hosea then is ordered to name his children according to this infidelity by giving them symbolic names (poor kids!). Eventually, though, Hosea takes Gomer back, and there is hope for a better relationship. The whole story serves as an analogy, what we scholars call a "prophetic sign-act," that represents God's relationship with the people. Just as Gomer cheated on Hosea, so have the people of Israel cheated on God. Just as Gomer suffers because of her infidelity, so will the people suffer. And just as Hosea takes back Gomer, so will God take back Israel.

Did God really order Hosea to marry an unfaithful woman just so that God could make a point? Or did Hosea find himself in a bad marriage and then think, "Hm, I can use this"? We have no way of knowing, and it doesn't really matter. What matters is the message of infidelity. Don't cheat on God.

By the way, the Bible loves marriage imagery for talking about the relationship between God and the people. Repeatedly, for instance, God is called the husband or bridegroom of Israel or the church. God is faithful; the people are unfaithful, but God persists in the relationship.

I can't help but point out that there is something sexist about this imagery. God is never the woman in the relationship but always the man, and it is the woman who is the "whore," the unfaithful one, not the man. The imagery is also heteronormative, meaning that it assumes a heterosexual relationship. Never in the Bible are God and the people described as a same-sex couple. Even so, the message about being faithful still rings out clearly.

If you don't believe in God, you can, once again, substitute Truth or Love for God and consider how to be faithful to those ideals.

Discussion

Hosea is using a dysfunctional relationship as an analogy for spiritual infidelity to God, but let's focus on human relationships for a moment. We humans are social creatures. We often commit ourselves to special individuals, but then we sometimes struggle to keep those commitments. How come, and what can we do to be more faithful?

For example, one challenge that marriages face—heterosexual or homosexual or any other kind of marriage—is that we humans often get a high from sexual and romantic passion, but that passion tends to diminish over time. Then we go searching for someone new who can give us that passion again. Some, including Einstein, have suggested that monogamy is unnatural (he cheated on his second wife regularly), that we humans are just not wired for having one partner for life. Yet we repeatedly try to find that one partner. We love the idea of discovering our soul mate, marrying our best friend, that one person unlike any other who can be the ultimate companion for us.

Is there a tug-of-war within us? One the one hand, we want multiple partners, but on the other, we want one? How do we resolve that? The Bible stresses fidelity to one partner. What challenges that fidelity, and what strengthens it?

My Suggested Bottom Line

The book of Hosea uses Hosea's dysfunctional marriage as an analogy for the troubled relationship between God and his people. The book can challenge us to think anew about fidelity.

Day Twenty-One: Jonah

Reading: The Book of Jonah

Background

Many of us scholars are confident that the book of Jonah is a work of fiction, but if you want to believe that it is factual, then go ahead. As always, what matters for our purposes is not "How did it happen?" but "What does it mean?"

This is a story that lots of people misunderstand because they focus on the wrong thing: the whale (or big fish; the ancient Israelites would not have differentiated between the two). Yes, at the end of Chapter One, Jonah is swallowed by a giant fish and lives inside it for three days until he is barfed up. That's an amusing part of the story that has captured the imaginations of Vacation Bible School programs everywhere. After all, children love animals, so we figure that this story about a guy inside a giant fish will be fun and engaging. And it is, but the whole fish part of the story is only one chapter out of four and misses the main point of the book of Jonah.

What really matters is *why* a giant fish swallows Jonah. He ends up in that great belly because he was trying to run away from God, who had commanded him to preach to the people of Nineveh, the capital of Assyria. We eventually learn that Jonah does not want to warn the Ninevites of God's wrath because he doesn't want to run the risk of those people repenting. You see, Jonah knows that, at heart, God is a softie, so if the Ninevites repent, God will forgive them and thus not punish them. Jonah wants them to be punished, so he doesn't want to preach to them.

Therefore, he foolishly runs away. The act is foolish because everyone knows you can't run away from God. Soon Jonah finds himself swallowed up by a giant fish, where he is forced to take a time-out and see the error of his ways. Once Jonah is barfed back up, he goes to Nineveh and warns them, just as he was supposed to in the first place.

Why does Jonah want Nineveh to be punished? As you know, Assyria was horrible to Israel, and Nineveh was the capital. Jonah wanting the Ninevites to suffer for their wrongdoings would be like Americans wanting the terrorists to suffer for having carried out 9–11. Most of us would not want God showing the terrorists mercy; likewise, Jonah does not want God showing the Ninevites mercy.

But God does. The Ninevites repent, even going so far as to have the animals wear sackcloth, the official biblical garment of repentance. So God decides not to punish them (3:10). Rather than being thankful for God's mercy, Jonah pouts. God sends a plant to give him shade from the hot, Middle Eastern sun while he pouts. Then God sends a worm to kill the plant, and Jonah sulks even more. Finally, God confronts Jonah, saying, basically, "You're all upset about the death of this plant. Shouldn't I care about all the people and animals of Nineveh?"

In other words, God cares about our enemies, so we should, too.

By the way, people often simplistically assert that the God of the Old Testament is wrathful while the God of the New Testament is merciful. The truth is more complicated. As you can see, the book of Jonah, which is in the Old Testament, is primarily about God showing mercy.

I was so taken with this message that, in 2010, I wrote and performed a thirty-minute, one-person play based on the book of Jonah called *Unother Nineveh* (available for your viewing pleasure on YouTube). I performed it for churches and anyone else who wanted to see it. That was a fun gig! I wrote it in response to some Islamophobic Christian group that was calling for the burning of Qur'ans. I wanted to amplify the message of showing mercy to people we think deserve punishment. My favorite character was the worm in Chapter Four. I loved wriggling around on the floor, pretending to be a worm (Seriously, who wouldn't want to do that?).

Discussion

Like it or not, showing mercy to our enemies is exactly what the book of Jonah is about. Not a giant fish and how amusing it is that a person was inside one. That's beside the point. No, the book of Jonah is about God showing mercy to people we hate, and the implied message is that we should show mercy to those people, too. Of course, we can protect ourselves from evil, but we are also to be open to mercy and forgiveness.

Again, forgiveness is tough. Some people are so horrible to us that it is understandable if we do not want to show mercy and forgiveness. So Jonah is quite challenging. How do we deal with this difficult teaching? How do we respect people's pain and not make light of the horrible things that one person does to another while also being open to showing mercy to our enemies?

For example, what about 9–11? What the hijackers did was inexcusable. Terrorism is barbaric. How do we show mercy to terrorists even while making clear that terrorism is unacceptable?

I have no easy answers here. I'm just responding to Jonah.

During World War II, a Japanese pastor named Kiyoshi Watanabe, who was fluent in English, was conscripted to serve as a translator at a camp in Hong Kong, where Japan was keeping British POW's. Watanabe soon observed that the British prisoners were not receiving adequate medical care. So then, even though the British were officially his enemies and even though he could be arrested (or worse) for treason, Watanabe began smuggling medication to the British POW's. He did similar acts of kindness for his enemies wherever he was stationed. Just as the government was getting wise to him, the war ended (In a painful twist of fate, Watanabe's wife and daughter were killed by the bombing of Hiroshima.).

Years later, Watanabe told his story on British television. The next day, a woman approached him. She told him that, because of the war, she had always hated the Japanese and had assumed that they were all simply evil. But now that she had heard Watanabe's story, she knew that the Japanese were capable of goodness, too.

Our enemies may do horrible things, but they are still people.

My Suggested Bottom Line

Jonah is about much more than a giant fish. It is primarily about the challenge of showing mercy to those who have done us terrible harm.

Day Twenty-Two: Mary

Reading: Luke 1:46–55

(Note: This is a New Testament passage.)

Background

I know, I know, this section is on the Old Testament, but Mary is in the New, so what's going on? Also, it might seem odd to read about Mary in a section on the prophets. We generally don't think of her as a prophet. I will say more about Mary in a later section, but I wanted to include her here precisely because, for most of us, she is not an obvious choice for a section on prophets.

She is not an obvious choice, but she definitely at least functions as a prophet in Luke 1 (which, again, is in the New Testament, not Old), where she utters her famous poem, the Magnificat. Again, prophets are intermediaries between God and the people who provide some sort of needed, and generally countercultural, message. Often that message is one of wrath, but it might be a word of mercy. The Magnificat is both. The poem offers a word of wrath to the wealthy and powerful while providing hope and comfort for the poor and oppressed, as we see in these verses: "[God] has shown strength with his arm; / he has scattered the proud in the thoughts of their hearts. / He has brought down the powerful from their thrones, / and lifted up the lowly; / he has filled the hungry with good things, / and sent the rich away empty" (vv. 51–53 NRSV). Like the prophets of the Old Testament, Mary presents a stern yet liberating word regarding socio-economic injustice, which is being realized through the baby she is carrying in her uterus.

Now, the point is not that it is inherently wrong to be proud, powerful, or wealthy. The real problem is that some people are those things while others are hungry and poor. In fact, in general, it is not pride, power, or wealth that the Bible condemns, but those qualities when they contribute to the suffering of others. Yes, pride is one of the seven deadly sins, but it is actually excessive pride that is the problem, what the ancient Greeks called "hubris." When pride becomes toxic, causing a person to make harmful choices, that is hubris, and that is what the Bible condemns. The Bible, including Mary, is not condemning self-confidence or having a positive self-esteem. The sin is in the excessive, destructive pride.

Regarding power and wealth, neither Mary's poem nor the Bible as a whole is condemning either. The Bible offers several positive examples of people wielding great power, such as King David, and the Bible sometimes presents wealth as a blessing, as it is for King Solomon. However, it is evident that, while God cares for all people, God has a special place in his heart for the poor and frequently warns the rich and powerful against the corruptive potential of wealth and power. Remember that 1 Timothy 6:10 warns, not that money is the root of all evil, but the *love of money* is a root of evil. Wealth and power tend to make us humans greedy; Mary and the Bible in general caution against wealth and power.

By contrast, Mary and the Bible as a whole offer sympathy and hope for the poor, but the idea is not that the poor are somehow inherently virtuous. Neither being poor nor being wealthy makes a person good or bad. The point simply is that the poor are at a severe disadvantage economically and so need help, but they also may be at an advantage over the wealthy because they are less likely to be seduced into idolatry by wealth.

Discussion

Do you consider yourself wealthy or poor? What do you do to keep yourself focused on helping others and not making your life all about money? What about power? Do you have a lot of power or a little? Are power and wealth relative terms? What do you do to keep yourself from abusing the power you have? What can you do to help liberate the less fortunate from systems that keep them oppressed?

My Suggested Bottom Line

The prophet Mary speaks wrath to the wealthy and powerful but liberation to the poor and weak.

Day Twenty-Three: Job

Introduction to Wisdom Literature
(Note: We are back in the Old Testament.)

For this topic we will look at what is often called Wisdom Literature, which refers to the poetic books that address the biblical understanding of wisdom. Wisdom Literature includes Psalms (some of them, at least), Proverbs, Ecclesiastes (called Qoheleth in Judaism), Song of Solomon (also called Song of Songs), and Job. What distinguishes these books is that they generally do not talk about Israel's history, including the Exodus, the monarchy, and the Exile. Instead, these books poetically focus on the key to, well, wisdom, which a person attains by following God. Here, wisdom is not about IQ or education but about revering God and modeling your life accordingly. As it says in Proverbs 1 (and elsewhere), "The fear of the Lord is the beginning of wisdom" (NRSV), with "fear" meaning awe and reverence for God. The wise person understands her or his place in the universe, which is important but is always subordinate to God.

Wisdom Literature addresses other themes, as well. It provides basic advice for good living in general, as we see in Proverbs. Sometimes contemporary readers incorrectly conclude that the advice in Proverbs is law that we must adhere to for all time. But the advice is just that, advice, which was given to particular people at a particular time. Just as we don't feel obligated always to follow "A penny saved is a penny earned" or "Birds of a feather flock together" or "Look before you leap," so also we need not feel obligated to follow the advice in Proverbs always. Proverbs provides guidance, not commands.

Wisdom Literature contains other themes, as well. Notably, it wrestles with big questions, especially why there is suffering if God is omnipotent (all-powerful) and wants to help us. Further, this literature sees God's wisdom embodied in nature, although Wisdom Literature is not promoting nature-worship or fixating on nature to the exclusion of attending services, studying Scripture, and helping the neighbor.

Fun fact: Wisdom Literature is not unique to the Bible. Other ancient civilizations, such as Egypt, had Wisdom Literature similar to what we see in the Bible. Actually, the writers of the Bible often borrowed from other cultures. For instance, the ancient Sumerians had an older flood story very similar to the story of Noah.

Reading: Job 1–2

Background

My mother, who was a far more devout Christian than I, hated the book of Job (pronounced Johb, not Jahb, by the way), and I can see why. What a brutal story! Job is wealthy and devoted to God. Satan, who here is not the evil, anti-God figure he is in the New Testament but is simply a member of God's court, argues that Job is faithful to God only because of all the wealth he has. If God took away all of Job's riches, Satan insists, Job would curse God. So God does something that I can't imagine the God I know would ever really do and that is allow Satan to bring pretty much every misery imaginable upon Job to see if he will then reject God. Job loses his wealth, all his family except for his wife, and is afflicted with boils. What Mom hated was the idea that God would play with someone's life like this. Fortunately, most of us scholars think this is a work of fiction that is trying to deal with the fact that sometimes good people suffer (theodicy).

It is an imprecise cliché to speak of the "patience of Job." Granted, he is patient in that he never turns his back on God, but, at the same time, Job becomes pretty fed-up with God (Who can blame him?). For most of the book's forty-two chapters, Job searches for an answer regarding why all this is happening but hears not a word from God until Chapter 38. Even then, God never does explain to Job why he is suffering—the reader knows about the deal with Satan, but Job never learns about that. Instead, God declares in an extensive, brutally poetic way, "I am God; you are a lowly human who doesn't know what he's talking about. Trust me." Then God restores to Job double of what he lost. So yes, Job is patient, but he grows furious with God, and I don't blame him.

I must confess that I think God is portrayed as a bit of a jerk in this book. There, I said it. I'm not saying that God is a jerk; I am commenting on the portrayal of God, not on God Godself. Not only does God bring misery upon Job, but then God is silent for most of the book. When God finally does answer, God harshly tells Job to shut up by saying, in essence, "I am God. I know better than you." So that's a non-answer. Thanks for nothing. Sure, God restores double what Job lost, but that doesn't undo all the terrible things that happened to him. I mean, he lost his children! If God took my children from me and then gave me new children, I would love them, but they wouldn't replace the ones God had killed. Ridiculous.

Job never learns why he suffered, but he does learn that his suffering was not a punishment. That's what his friends tell him, that his suffering is due to him having done something wrong. God makes clear that such is not the case. So while the book does not provide solid answers regarding suffering in the world, it does underscore that suffering is not always karmic. In fact, the irony is that Job's suffering is due to his righteousness, not his sinfulness.

Discussion

What do you make of the book of Job? Does it bother you as much as it bothers me? Is God a jerk in this book?

Among other things, the book is struggling with the unfairness of life. Does the book offer guidance for how you can help someone who is going through a rough time? A mistake Job's friends make is that they say that his suffering is a punishment. People often think that about their suffering, so this book could help us to guide people away from such thinking.

My Suggested Bottom Line

The book of Job ponders the reality of suffering, making the point that there is not a tidy relationship between our conduct and reward/suffering. Sometimes good people suffer for reasons we will never know (just as Job never knows).

Day Twenty-Four: Psalm 13

Reading: Psalm 13

Background

The Psalms are beloved, the darlings of the Bible. People find them easy to understand and full of emotions and thoughts that many of us can relate to. The Psalms are also appealing because they are usually short, and they are, of course, poetic. If you read only the Psalms and noting else in the Bible, you would miss out on a lot, but you would also have plenty to nourish you all the days of your life.

Contrary to popular belief, the Psalms were probably not written by David. Actually, David's name appears in the heading of only seventy-three out of the one hundred-fifty psalms, and his name does not necessarily indicate authorship but could simply mean that the psalm is in honor of David or in the style of David or in accord with the Davidic line. On the other seventy-seven psalms, we have other names listed at the top, such as Asaph and Korah. There is even a psalm of Moses and a psalm of Solomon. Finally, there are quite a few psalms with no one's name attached. However, if, at the end of it all, you insist on attributing the Psalms to David, that's fine. When it comes to the Bible, authorship is often a battle not worth fighting because what matters is what the passage says, not who wrote it. I mean, occasionally authorship matters, but generally it does not.

These one hundred-fifty psalms, which were the hymns of the Temple, come in different types. Some offer thanksgiving for God having done a wondrous deed. Some psalms simply praise God without focusing on giving thanks for anything in particular. There are psalms that recount great events. There are psalms that were clearly for special occasions; for instance, Psalm 2 was obviously used whenever Israel crowned a new king. Psalm 119, the longest psalm at 176 verses, is a meditation on the value of studying God's teachings. Psalm 23, the most famous of the group, is a confidence psalm in that it expresses trust in God even during difficult times.

Then there are the laments, of which Psalm 13 is an excellent example. The ancient Israelites were geniuses at lamenting, expressing sorrow as part of their communal worship experience. In fact, the Bible has an entire book devoted to the practice called, not surprisingly, Lamentations. For the ancient Israelites, it was acceptable to express sorrow, grief, and even anger to God; the psalms of lament provided an official way to do that during worship.

Psalm 13, with its raw bluntness but also with its ultimate expression of hope and gratitude, is a typical lament. The speaker starts off with poignant frankness: "How long, O LORD? Will you / forget me forever?" And the psalmist isn't quick to let up. Four out of the psalm's six verses are a cry of sorrow. The psalmist even orders God: "Consider and answer me, O LORD / my God! / Give light to my eyes, or I will / sleep the sleep of death . . . " (v. 3 NRSV).

The last two verses abruptly shift to gratitude, as laments often do. Did the psalmist receive some answer to her or his lament, or is she or he just being hopeful that all will work out well? In either case, we have a resolution of confidence, but not first without unflinching sorrow.

Implied in this psalm and the laments in general is that sometimes good people experience horrible things. This idea runs counter to the idea that we see in other parts of the Bible, such as the book of Deuteronomy or even in other psalms (Psalm 1, for example), that the good are rewarded and the bad are punished. After all, there is nothing in Psalm 13 that indicates that the speaker is suffering because God is punishing her or him for wrongdoing.

We don't know why the speaker is suffering, and it doesn't matter. The point is that she or he is suffering, is expressing sorrow openly to God, and is going to be rescued by God.

My students often say that they believe in karma, the Eastern idea of "what comes around goes around," that you will be rewarded or punished according to your actions. Parts of the Bible agree with this idea, too (even though the word "karma" does not appear in the Bible), but other parts of the Bible, including much of the Wisdom Literature, challenge this belief that you reap what you sow.

Discussion

What do you think of Psalm 13? Do you like the idea of lamenting to God? When can we incorporate lamentation into our society, even for those who do not believe in God? After all, we can still lament our situation even if our complaints are not directed at a deity. Do we have lamentation built into our society already? Do we try to avoid public and communal lamentation? When can lamenting go too far? Are we Americans afraid to get together as a group and lament, or are we comfortable with the practice?

My Suggested Bottom Line

Psalm 13 shows that lament is an acceptable part of public, communal worship. God can handle our sorrow and anger.

Day Twenty-Five: Psalm 23

Reading: Psalm 23

Background

This is *the* Psalm, the one that even people who never attend synagogue or church at least have heard of. Because it is so familiar, I contemplated not including it in this book. Then again, it is often the hyper-familiar that we know the least well because our overexposure frequently begets dismissal. Psalm 23 comes along, and we think, "Yeah, yeah, been there, done that. I know this psalm, so I can tune out." So then, I included the psalm, as well as some other hyper-familiar biblical passages, precisely because we think we know them better than we actually do.

This is a confidence or trust psalm. It does not lament misfortune, nor does it praise God for anything so much as it asserts faith in God's care for us.

The psalm opens with a shepherd metaphor, the shepherd having been a common vocation in ancient Israel and also a metaphor for the king. Implicitly, we readers and reciters of the psalm are the sheep. People often make much of the sheep's reputation for low intelligence, but nothing is made of that trait here. Rather, we are reassured that God is with us to take care of us, even when are going through the darkest valley.

What people often seem to miss is that, starting in verse five, the sheep/shepherd metaphor is replaced with banquet and house images of God caring for the people through food and oil and safety. In a way, actually, verses five and six convey the same basic messages as in the first four verses but in a different way: God will take care of you.

Note that both parts of the psalm acknowledge that bad will happen. The psalm is not saying, "Nothing bad will ever happen to you" but instead is asserting, "When bad things happen to you, God will be there to help you."

Christians debate whether the last line of the psalm should be translated as "I shall dwell in the house of / the LORD / my whole life long" or "I shall dwell in the house of / the LORD / forevermore." Many Christians prefer the latter because it seems to reinforce the idea of eternal life, but the former is probably more accurate. After all, in the Old Testament, you don't really find the idea of eternal life. The Old Testament focuses on God blessing us and caring for us in this life, not the next. But regardless of which ending you go with, the basic meaning of the psalm is the same.

If you believe in God, this psalm can be quite comforting. If you don't believe in God, perhaps, again, you can insert "Truth" or "Love" in place of "God."

Discussion

How specifically does God (or Truth or Love) shepherd us, feed us, and protect us? The imagery of this psalm is lovely, but what does it really mean? What does it mean to say that God makes us lie down in green pastures and leads us beside still waters? What does all that look like in our daily lives?

How can we imitate the Shepherd by being like little shepherds (shepherdettes?) to one another? How can you, for instance, lead others beside still waters and make them lie down in green pastures? How can this psalm be a guide for us on caring for others?

My Suggested Bottom Line

Psalm 23 expresses confidence that God will help us.

Day Twenty-Six: Psalm 137

Reading: Psalm 137

Background

Among the psalms, this is the lament of laments, so much so that it is seldom used in worship, at least in Christianity. The psalm references the Exile, that event in which a large portion of the people of Judah (Southern Israel) were kept in captivity in Babylon until they were liberated by the Persians. In Psalm 137, the speaker laments that it is impossible to sing about Jerusalem, Zion (an important hill in Jerusalem), home, in this foreign land where oppressors mock God's people. The speaker declares that her or his tongue should stick to the roof of her or his mouth for failing to remember Jerusalem.

Then we come to the curse in the last three verses of the psalm. The world of the Bible featured both blessings and curses. Pronouncing one of those on someone was serious business. A curse or blessing was binding. Here, the speaker asks God to remember the Edomites, a neighboring people who took advantage of Judah when it fell to the Babylonians. Then we come to the curse the speaker pronounces upon the Babylonians: "Happy shall they be who pay / you back / what you have done to us! / Happy shall they be who take / your little ones / and dash them against a rock! (vv. 8b-9 NRSV). This savage language makes this psalm a challenge to use in worship, where we generally try to speak in positive, uplifting ways and call on people to love their enemies.

On second thought, though, I suspect many people in the pew could probably identify with this psalm. Truth be told, we humans often secretly or overtly long for our enemies to suffer a brutal fate. Think about how much fury we Americans have against ISIS and other terrorist groups who appear to delight in brutally killing innocent people. We even lash out viciously at people who are guilty of far less. Think about how often on social media we read horrible messages that call for people to die a miserable death simply because they voted for a particular candidate or believe in the separation of church and state. I wish I could say that Christians don't stoop to such a level, but sadly they are among the worst offenders.

I keep wondering why that is. Here is a religion that features this gentle Jesus who emphasizes love and helping those in need, yet Christianity, at least in the United States, is often dominated by nastiness. Christians are notorious for being self-righteous and intolerant. Of course, there are legions of Christians who are not like that, so maybe part of the problem is that the noisiest, most obnoxious Christians get all the media coverage. In any case, if being honest, quite a few Christians would acknowledge that they can identify with Psalm 137's horrific last lines.

If you are going to make sense of the Bible, you need to understand each passage in the context of the Bible as a whole. Psalm 137 is a raw call for the bloody death of the enemy's babies, but the Bible as a whole does not call for us to hate and wish violence upon our enemies. Remember that Jesus says in Matthew 5:44, "Love your enemies, and pray for those who persecute you." Or think again of the book of Jonah, which emphasizes showing mercy to those who wrong us. There are other passages in the Bible that glorify the slaughter of our enemies, but the overall message is one of peace, love, and forgiveness.

Discussion

What do we do with Psalm 137 and other violent passages in the Bible? What does Psalm 137 say to you? Do you see it as allowing for people to give voice to their pain? How does the psalm square with passages in the Bible that call for people to love and forgive their enemies? Or maybe you can't forgive someone, but does that mean it is acceptable to wish horrifying suffering and death to befall that person?

How do we deal with the furious sorrow that some people's barbaric actions elicit from us?

My Suggested Bottom Line

Psalm 137 is a savage lament that gives voice to the desire for revenge we humans often feel when someone does terrible harm to us.

Day Twenty-Seven: Proverbs

Reading: Proverbs 9

Background

The book of Proverbs is a collection of advice probably originally intended for young men before they headed into the world. We are told at the beginning that these are the "proverbs of Solomon," but many of us scholars think that this book was written long after the time of Solomon. Perhaps the book reflects wisdom passed down from him. It's hard to say, and, for our purposes, it doesn't really matter.

The book contains two types of sayings. One is the short saying, a pithy bit of advice often set up in two lines that parallel each other somehow. Consider, for instance, Proverbs 6:20: "My child, keep your father's / commandment, / and do not forsake your / mother's teaching." This verse obviously stresses the importance of listening to one's parents by essentially saying the same thing in two different ways. So then, we are not to read too much into "commandment" being associated with "your father" and "teaching" associated with "your mother." The point is to listen to your parents, period. The parallelism[1] of the two parts of the verse is a poetic device that underscores the point. Some popular themes among these sayings are warnings against laziness, greed, foolish talk, and immoral women, as well as encouraging people to work hard, be slow to speak, and associate with upright people. Above

---

1. By the way, parallelism is a common device in biblical poetry.

all, always be humbly devoted to God, including by learning from God's teachings.

The other type of saying in the book of Proverbs is the longer poem, most notably the passages on Woman Wisdom, the personification of God's wisdom. Proverbs 8 and 9 go on at length about her and her opposite, Woman Foolishness. She is not the same as God, for God created her, but she is with God during creation and calls us away from arrogance, foolish talk, and other behaviors that lead to misery. Again, it is striking that, despite the Bible's focus on male language for God, here we have at least God's wisdom personified as a woman.

Discussion

As we see in Proverbs 9, at least at first glance Woman Wisdom and Woman Foolishness look and sound the same. How do we tell the difference between wisdom and foolishness?

What are some manifestations of foolishness? One that I think of is stubbornness in the face of truth or commonsense. Sometimes we humans cling to our beliefs no matter what anyone says. We have our version of the truth, and we don't want to be open even a bit to the possibility that we might be wrong. Are you ever like that? How can we correct ourselves so that we are not like that? Is there any guidance from the book of Proverbs along those lines?

What are other ways that we humans are foolish, and what does Proverbs offer to help us be wiser, even if we are not religious?

Finally, let me underline a point I made earlier: do not think that Proverbs is a rulebook for life that we must adhere to rigidly. It is a collection of advice, but that advice was given to particular people in specific circumstances. Of course, there is something timeless about Proverbs, but finding timeless truths in Proverbs does not demand following Proverbs like it is the absolute rulebook for life that we must adhere to without consideration of context.

My Suggested Bottom Line

Proverbs offers guidance for good living, including through its depiction of Woman Wisdom.

Day Twenty-Eight: Ecclesiastes/ Qoheleth

Reading: Ecclesiastes 1, 3:1-8

Background

This is such a strange book to find in the Bible. It is a dissenting voice, the perfect example of this self-criticism built into the Old Testament. Much of the Bible, not surprisingly, calls readers to follow God's commandments and learn God's wisdom. Doing so will lead to a life of blessing, even if not a life immune from suffering. But then in walks Ecclesiastes, which declares that pursuing wisdom and trying to do right are just a big waste of time. "Vanity of vanities!" we hear in the second verse of the book. "What do people gain from all / the toil / at which they toil under the / sun?" we hear in verse three. In verses thirteen and fourteen, we hear the "Teacher . . . applied my mind to seek and search out by wisdom all that is done under heaven . . . I saw all the deeds that are done under the sun, and see, all is vanity and a chasing after wind" (NRSV).

In Chapter Two, the Teacher speaks of his great accomplishments and how pointless they are and then recommends that the only thing worth doing is just enjoying life, including "toil." But then he goes on to talk about how miserable and pointless all our work is. Ultimately the book affirms that we should trust in God and get as much out of life as we can, but the book repeatedly undercuts its own message with its steady drumbeat about the futility and unfairness of life.

By far, the most famous passage in Ecclesiastes is 3:1-8, in which we read that there is a time for everything, good and bad. Some of you may recall that, in the 1960s, the Byrds performed a song based on this passage. I have heard this passage read at funerals, although I do not find it comforting to hear, for example, that there is "a time to kill" (v. 3 NRSV), "a time to hate" and "a time for war" (v. 8 NRSV). This gets read at funerals to assure people that death is just a part of life, but these verses make it sound like suffering and misery are all part of God's plan, an idea that makes God sound sadistic or at least insensitive. Anyway, whatever comfort these verses may provide is short-lived, because verses nine and following get right back into the pointlessness of it all.

Ecclesiastes is a messy book defying easy answers. It ultimately affirms following God and embracing life, but it is unflinching in its acknowledgement that much of life appears to be absurd. It's as if the book is here to say, "Pursue wisdom, but don't expect that you will always find it. The wise person knows that wisdom is, to a degree, elusive."

On a different but related note, when I was in the parish, I often heard a kind of lamenting about how awful the present times are and how better things used to be back in the Day. Such talk would remind me of Ecclesiastes 7:10: "Do not say, 'Why were the / former days better than / these? / For it is not from wisdom that / you ask this.'" At the same time, I tried to empathize with people as they expressed their concerns. Change is hard, and it is easy to get anxious about societal shifts.

Discussion

What do you make of this book? What's the point?

One idea that comes to mind is that the book, like some others, provides a dissenting voice that challenges the Bible's prevailing wisdom. Does the presence of Ecclesiastes in the Bible teach us the value of including dissenting voices in our discussions? It is easy for us to surround ourselves with people who think like us, but what are the benefits of including at least one person who can challenge us?

Another thought I have has to do with Ecclesiastes 3:1-8, which says there is a designated time for everything. I frequently hear people say, "Everything happens for a reason," a statement, as I mentioned, that I often find troubling because it seems to make light of suffering. For instance, when my mother died suddenly on December 21, 2010, if you had said to me, "Everything happens for a reason," I would have been furious with you. As I sat at her funeral on December 27, I found myself not wanting to be there and not wanting reassurance from some pastor. I just wanted my mom back. So we need to be careful and sensitive about saying "Everything happens for a reason."

Ecclesiastes 3 says there is a time for everything, which is not the same as saying everything happens for a reason, but it does suggest a larger design to the universe. Do you think there is a larger design to the universe? Do you think some things are fate? Can you believe that there is this larger design even if you don't believe in God?

Finally, Ecclesiastes both stresses the importance of enjoying life and also the painful futility of life. What do you think of that? Do you agree? Can we both enjoy life while also seeing it as futile?

My Suggested Bottom Line

Ecclesiastes offers a challenging description of life as painful and futile but also encourages us to enjoy life and trust in God.

Day Twenty-Nine: Song of Solomon

Reading: Song of Solomon 1

Background

Today we are looking at Song of Solomon, also called Song of Songs. Like Esther, this book never mentions God yet implies God all throughout. The book is unique in the Bible in that it is a collection of love poems between a man and a woman. Many readers think that the man is King Solomon. There is no solid proof for that, but think what you want. Most of us scholars contend that this book was written long after Solomon's death, but again, I'm not sure it matters whom we ascribe the book to.

Of special note is the prominence of the woman, whom I call SongWoman, in this erotic book. She speaks first. She expresses love and passion and sexual desire just as freely and openly as the man does. When he goes missing in Chapters Three and Five, she ventures into the streets at night in search of him, risking her safety in the process. She and the man appear to be equals in this relationship. Once again, we see in the Bible, which is full of male dominance, an example of defiance against that dominance. The fact that this book is *the* Song of Songs, suggesting that it is the ultimate song, implies that this portrayal of equality is an ideal.

Of course, SongWoman would be even more powerful if she didn't fixate so much on having a man in her life. If she were more independent, she would be an even stronger model. Nevertheless, Song of Solomon presents us with a relationship in which there is mutual respect and adoration. The woman is not inferior to the man, and she is just as free to express her sexuality as he is, an important point given that historically women have often been told to suppress their sexuality.

Many readers interpret Song of Solomon as an extended metaphor or allegory for the relationship between God and God's people. God loves us just as these two people love each other. That interpretation has value, but it is important not to skip over the fact that this book, first and foremost, is a celebration of sexual, romantic love between two people.

I once had a student in my catechism class say, "Sex is sinful." I don't know if he was just saying what he thought the pastor wanted to hear, but his words reflect a longstanding notion in Christianity that sex is inherently dirty (No wonder some people refer to their genitals as "junk" and sex as "doing the nasty."). Song of Solomon celebrates sexual love and eroticism. There is nothing dirty about sex. God invented the orgasm! But we are to be careful with our sexual intimacy so that God and other people are honored in the process. When sex hurts others or ourselves, we have a tragic problem.

Discussion

According to Song of Solomon, what makes for a good, healthy romantic and sexual relationship? Why do relationships often go bad? Women frequently get treated as sex objects and as inferior to men; how can we fix that in our relationships? How do we allow women to enjoy their sexuality without reducing them to sexual objects?

Song of Solomon is about a heterosexual relationship, but what about a homosexual one? What lessons can we apply from Song of Solomon to any romantic relationship?

My Suggested Bottom Line

Song of Solomon describes an erotic romance that puts the man and woman on equal terms and celebrates human sexuality.

Part Two

The New Testament

Day Thirty: Mary and Joseph

Reading: Matthew 1:18-25, Luke 1:26-38

Background

We have now crossed (pun intended) into the New Testament. Just to refresh your memory, the New Testament deals with Jesus and the early church, while the Old Testament comes before all that. Christians actually borrowed the Old Testament from the Jews. So then, the Old Testament is common to Christians and Jews, while the New Testament is Scripture only for Christians.

Doubtless some readers will complain that I don't spend enough time on Jesus and the New Testament. They may be right, but I spent more time on the Old Testament for the simple reason that it is considerably longer and, in many ways, more complex.

The first four books of the New Testament, Matthew, Mark, Luke, and John, are gospels (a word that literally means "good news"), which in this case are accounts of the life of Jesus of Nazareth, who lived in Israel two thousand years ago and who Christians believe to be the Messiah, that is, the one anointed by God to save God's people and whose coming is prophesied in the Old Testament. Jews generally do not believe that Jesus is the Messiah, and, unlike most Christians, they certainly do not believe that he is divine.

By the way—and I cannot stress this enough—it is profoundly tragic and vile that the New Testament has been used to justify anti-Semitism. There is no place for such repulsive nonsense.

Jesus himself was Jewish, as were many of his followers, and the Bible makes clear that the Jews are to be respected as God's Chosen People. Some of Jesus' opponents were Jewish, but some were not. Moreover, in general, the Bible stresses love over hate when it comes to all people, including those who are different from us.

The readings I selected for today tell of the birth of Jesus, but I chose them because they focus on Mary and Joseph, Jesus' mother and stepfather. Later, I will reflect on the birth stories themselves, but right now I want to highlight Mary and Joseph. Luke puts the spotlight on Mary, Matthew on Joseph.

How do these passages depict Mary and Joseph? Mary comes across as both obedient and, as I mentioned, prophetic. When the angel announces to her that she is going to be the biological mother of the Messiah, she asks how exactly that will happen, but she also expresses receptivity to the calling. Her acceptance of her new task is striking because frequently, in call-stories, the hero initially rejects the call or expresses doubt about his or her ability to live up to it. Mary does neither. Her asking about how she can be a mother when she is a virgin is not doubt so much as it is an effort to understand better what is going to happen. Never does she express anything along the lines of "I can't do that," as, for instance, Moses does in Exodus when God calls him. She doesn't run the other way like Jonah. She doesn't later prove disappointing, like Peter. No, Mary accepts the call and, as we see later in the gospels, never fails to carry it out. She is even present at Jesus' crucifixion, at least according to John's gospel.

Joseph is likewise obedient. In Matthew's gospel, Joseph repeatedly does what he is supposed to do in the face of difficult circumstances. When he finds out that Mary is pregnant but doesn't know yet that the pregnant is miraculous, Joseph resolves to break off their betrothal quietly, thereby rejecting the punishment for adultery, stoning. Then an angel tells him in a dream about the child and orders him to marry Mary, so Joseph does so. Later, after Jesus is born, when Joseph is warned in a dream that Jesus' life is in jeopardy, Joseph takes child and Mary and flees to Egypt for refuge, where he remains until he is told again that it is safe to return.

Like Mary, Joseph does not question his call or express doubt in his ability to do it. He just does it.

The point is not that a person cannot express doubt about her or his ability to carry out a call. After all, Moses does so, and there are few people in the Bible greater than Moses. But that they do not express doubt about their ability to carry out the call is commendable of Mary and Joseph and something for us to strive for.

By the way, there has been much discussion about how old Mary and Joseph were and whether they had any children of their own and also what ended up happening to Joseph, who disappears from the gospels shortly after Jesus is born. You may certainly explore all that, but I am not going to here. My focus is simply on what the Bible says and what that means for us, not on the logistics of Mary and Joseph's marriage, which the Bible doesn't bother with.

Discussion

We talked about call before, but let's visit it again since it is central to how we humans think of ourselves. The concept of call is prevalent among Christians and Jews, but it is relevant to all of us. Anyone can be called to a task, whether by God, other people, or circumstances. A pastoral colleague of mine once said that he didn't know if God was calling him to be a pastor, but he knew the church was. Calls can come from anywhere.

Four years ago, July 15, 2015, I took my then twenty-two-year-old daughter, Katie, to the doctor because she had been nauseated. She had had stomach trouble before, in large part because of not eating right, so that's what we thought was the culprit this time. Katie just needed to eat better.

The PA said, "Let's do a pregnancy test, just to rule that out."

Katie said, "There's no way I can be pregnant, but OK."

Ten minutes later, the PA returned. "Well, I guess congratulations are in order."

Katie was horrified. She did not want to have a child. She and her boyfriend were ill with dread. My wife, Kim, and I felt sorry for them, even though we were also annoyed with them for not having been more careful so as to prevent pregnancy in the first place. But, as Dr. Phil says, "Sometimes you make the right decision, and sometimes you make the decision right." My daughter and her boyfriend accepted the call to parenthood, even though they were terrified, and Kim and I accepted the call to grandparenthood, even though we really didn't want to be grandparents.

Of course, four years later, I adore my granddaughter, Mle (pronounced "Emily"). I was honored to be with my daughter when she delivered. Mle is a hilarious and loving child whom I take great delight in helping raise. When she sees me and raises her arms to me to indicate that she wants me to pick her up, my heart melts every single time. Being a grandparent has never been a goal of mine, but this is the calling, so I am doing it and loving it.

What about you? What calls do you have? What have you been called to that maybe you didn't want to do? Did you respond like Moses or like Mary and Joseph? What can we learn from Mary and Joseph about how to respond to a call with acceptance? In general, what can we learn from the call stories in the Bible?

My Suggested Bottom Line

Mary and Joseph heroically embrace their calling to be the parents of Jesus.

Day Thirty-One: Peter and Mary Magdalene

Reading: Matthew 14:22-33, John 20:1-18

Background

P eter is generally regarded as the head of the apostles, the inner circle of Jesus' closest followers. Mary Magdalene is frequently regarded as his female counterpart among the women disciples, in part because in lists of women disciples, she is often first. She also has a special encounter with the risen Jesus in John 20 that no one else has, male or female.

Peter, whose name means "rock" and who also is known as "Simon" (and "Cephas" in Paul's letters) is portrayed in the gospels as well-meaning but bumbling. We can see those two sides of his nature in the reading from Matthew that I selected for today. When Peter sees Jesus walking on the water, he asks if he can join Jesus. Jesus says yes. At first, Peter is able to walk on the water, too, but then he looks away from Jesus and starts to sink. Jesus rescues him but chides him a bit for doubting. So initially Peter does something amazing, walks on the water, but then screws it up. Typical Peter.

Of course, Peter's biggest blunder is his denial of Jesus. Even though Peter vows that he will never deny him, a few hours later he does just that. That's our Peter: full of good intentions but not always great about follow-through. Granted, he's no Judas Iscariot, who betrays Jesus. Still, in the gospels, Peter fails repeatedly.

Despite his shortcomings, however, Jesus entrusts to him the "keys to the kingdom of heaven" and declares that Peter is a rock on which Jesus will build his church. What Jesus means by that exactly has been up for debate, but the bottom line is that Jesus does not give up on Peter. Peter can still do great things despite his flaws. Indeed, he would go on to be one of the great leaders of the church. In Roman Catholicism, he was the first pope.

In fact, we see Peter do great things in the book of Acts, the fifth book of the New Testament and the sequel to the gospel of Luke. Starting in Acts 2, at the story of Pentecost, Peter is a confident and articulate leader who addresses thousands of people to explain the Pentecost miracle of people suddenly being able to speak other languages. Throughout the book of Acts, Peter is a strong champion of Christianity who can even do miracles. From a Christian standpoint, we would say that Peter grows because the Spirit guides him, but whether you believe in God or not, you can still find encouragement in Peter's story of going from well-meaning but inept to bold and capable.

Mary Magdalene's story does not contain this path of growth because she never bumbles; in fact, none of the women disciples do. Repeatedly in the gospels, the women do better than the men when it comes to following Jesus. As we see in our reading from John, yes, Mary Magdalene doesn't recognize Jesus at first, but that failure to recognize him does not appear to be a problem. Once she does recognize him, she is as devout and loving as anyone could be. There is also the fact that she is able to have this encounter with the risen Jesus because she is at the tomb, whereas no one else is, including Peter. Jesus then sends her to tell the others that she has seen him. In fact, she is often called "The Apostle to the Apostles," since she was sent by Jesus to tell the others and the word "apostle" means "one who is sent."

One of the main stories about Mary Magdalene isn't about her per se but about how Christians have characterized her. She is widely regarded as having been a prostitute who gave up that profession to follow Jesus. She is also sometimes thought of as Jesus' lover or even wife. She may have been all of those things, but the

Bible does not say any of that. The Bible says that she had seven demons that Jesus had driven out of her, but it never says that she was a prostitute, let alone a love interest for Jesus.

Discussion

Mary Magdalene's role among Jesus' disciples underscores the importance and prominence of women for the Jesus movement. Indeed, there is quite a bit of evidence indicating that, in the early years of Christianity, women played important roles, including as leaders. Her dedication to Jesus and her leadership challenge us to include women in such positions. Break the stained glass ceiling. How do we exclude women? How do we unfairly sexualize them, just as Christians have long done to Mary Magdalene, and how can we fix that?

Peter's story offers hope for us that, like him, we can get it together. Just as Peter needs the Holy Spirit and Jesus' help, so we might need help, but we can rise to greater success. How do we get in our own way? When do we speak or act impetuously in a bad way, as Peter often does? What can we learn from Peter about dealing with mistakes and growing? Just as Peter gets help from God toward growth, what or who can help you grow?

My Suggested Bottom Line

Mary Magdalene's leadership highlights the importance of women while Peter's transformation presents hope to all of us as we struggle with our shortcomings.

Day Thirty-Two: John the Baptist

Reading: Mark 6:17-29

Background

J ohn the Baptist is like an Old Testament prophet who wandered into the New Testament. Actually, with his clothing of camel's hair and a leather belt around his waist, he calls to mind Elijah, who 2 Kings 1:8 describes as "hairy . . . with a leather belt around his waist" (NRSV). John the Baptist is a rugged man who lives in the wilderness on locusts and wild honey and who preaches a harsh message of repentance, calling the Pharisees and Sadducees a "brood of vipers" (Matthew 3:7 NRSV). As we see in the readings from Luke, John the Baptist's call is to prepare the way for the coming of the Messiah, Jesus, who, according to Luke, is six months younger than John and is a relative. John the Baptist also baptizes Jesus, a task he does not feel worthy of according to Matthew 3:14, in which John suggests that Jesus should actually baptize him, not the other way around.

By the way, one question Christians have often pondered is, if baptism washes away sin and if Jesus is without sin (both of those premises are supported by the Bible), then why does Jesus need to be baptized? One explanation is that Jesus is setting an example for the rest of us. Another is that the baptism serves to mark the beginning of his public ministry; it is a kind of coronation or inauguration. I don't know the answer, but I lean toward the latter because of the reference in the baptismal account to Psalm 2, which was used in ancient Israel for coronations. What do you think?

Then we come to our reading from Mark, which tells of John the Baptist's death. It is astounding how twisted this story is. Herod, a king almost always associated with evil in the gospels, has had John arrested because he had criticized Herod's marriage to Herodias, so Herodias now has a grudge against him. At a birthday banquet, Herod's daughter dances for the guests, and Herod is so pleased that he promises in front of everyone to give the girl whatever she wants. After consulting with her mother, she asks for John the Baptist's head on a platter. Although not wanting to go through with the request since he actually somewhat likes and fears John, Herod grants the wish. So here we have a mother and father involving their daughter in a horrifying act of killing a person and then carrying that person's head. That girl is going to need some serious therapy.

Sadly, a theme in the Bible is that great servants of God often die a terrible death, including, of course, Jesus himself. But then, throughout history we have seen that pursuing a noble cause frequently comes at a great price.

Discussion

John the Baptist speaks a harsh word to try to persuade people to pull their act together. When do we need to speak a harsh word? What is the right and wrong way to do that? Ephesians 4:15 advises us to speak "the truth in love." How do we do that? What issues call for a John the Baptist approach, and what should we let go?

It is important to add that speaking a harsh word never means insulting or demeaning people. We are to speak the truth in love, not in hate.

A second relevant discussion topic is preparation. John the Baptist's job is to prepare people for the coming of Jesus by baptizing them and getting them to "bear fruit worthy of repentance" (Matt 3:8 NRSV). In other words, clean up your act. What big events or people do we need to prepare for, and how do we clean up our act in the name of preparation?

Another relevant discussion topic pertains to John the Baptist's death. For starters, the story shows a child being pulled into a horrifically adult situation. The episode reminds me of how important it is not to involve children with adult problems if possible and not to use them as pawns for our own agenda, as parents often do, such as when they are fighting. The people of biblical times did not have the same understanding of childhood that we have, but there is no denying that this child is being placed in a ghastly situation by corrupt people who have little regard for her well-being.

For that matter, we shouldn't do this to adults either, triangulate them into some toxic situation for our selfish gain.

Of course, even worse off is John the Baptist himself, who ends up dead because he criticized Herod and Herodias for their marriage. While you and I are not likely to behead someone who criticizes us (I hope), the story nevertheless can challenge us to rethink how we respond to criticism. Will we respond in a mature, non-anxious manner, or will we respond with cruel lashing out? Also, what happens when we are the giver of the criticism, as John is here? There are times when we need to speak a critical word; we need to be ready for the consequences, which could be severe.

Another topic for discussion could be about Herod's conduct as king. He makes an extravagant promise that he ends up regretting. How easy it is for us to get caught up in a moment and say or do things that will haunt us later. How can we protect ourselves from Herod behavior?

My Suggested Bottom Line

John the Baptist is a courageous teller of the truth who pays horribly for doing so.

Day Thirty-Three: The Birth of Jesus

Reading: Matthew 2, Luke 2

Background

The two accounts of Jesus' birth contradict each other on several points, but the contradiction does not matter since our focus is on what the stories mean and not what actually happened. Luke's account is the better known of the two and is the one you are most likely to hear read on Christmas Eve. It tells of the census that requires Mary and Joseph to travel from Nazareth to Bethlehem, where they stay in a manger because there is no room for them in the inn. Then the shepherds visit them that night after Mary gives birth to Jesus. Christmas pageants and nativity scenes often depict this event with great sentimentality and several animals.

Matthew's account is more ominous. It contains no mention of a census or journey from Nazareth to Bethlehem. Instead, it seems that Mary and Joseph live in Bethlehem since there is no mention of them traveling there and since they are in a house when the magi visit them. Those magi—no shepherds—arrive from the East by following a star. They stop to ask King Herod for directions. When Herod hears of a new king being born, he panics (and all of Jerusalem with him, the verse says). He sends the magi on, requesting that they report back to him the location of the baby so that he may "pay homage" as well. Of course, what he really wants to do is kill the baby. The magi make their visit—by the way, the Bible does not tell us how many magi there are—and they present

Jesus with gifts of gold, frankincense, and myrrh (If Jesus was like every other baby, then he probably tried to put all three of these gifts into his mouth.). The magi are warned not to return to Herod, so they go home by another means. When Herod finds out that the magi have eluded him, he becomes enraged and orders the killing of all boys two years old and younger in Bethlehem. This horrible event is known as the Murder of the Holy Innocents and is commemorated on December 28, during the twelve days of Christmas. An angel warns Joseph in a dream to flee, so he, Mary, and Jesus escape Israel and live as refugees in Egypt until Joseph is told in another dream that it is safe to return.

Luke's gospel also has the only account in the Bible of Jesus as a child beyond infancy. When he is twelve, he and some family travel to Jerusalem. While there, Jesus wanders off and joins up with some religion scholars, whom the boy Jesus starts to teach. As they are heading home, Mary and Joseph discover that Jesus is missing. They frantically return to Jerusalem to search for him. When they find him, Jesus quips that they should have known that he would be in his Father's house, that is, the Temple (I still would have grounded him.).

Discussion

Again, try not to worry about what really happened historically. We don't know. As many a pageant and nativity scene demonstrate, people often conflate the two accounts so that, for example, we end up with shepherds and magi standing side-by-side at the manger, even though the Bible never gives us such a scene (I sound like a lot of fun at Christmastime, don't I?). I encourage you not to blur these stories together. Treat them separately. After all, that was how they were written. Matthew's account and Luke's account, before they ended up in the Bible, circulated independently of each other. Matthew did not write, "For more on the birth, see Luke," and vice versa.

So then, let's treat each version independently. What does Matthew's version suggest about Jesus and his birth? What is the significance of magi visiting him? Magi, by the way, were scholars who studied the stars, and these men (assuming they were men; maybe they weren't), being from the East, are from outside Israel and so are not Jews. They are foreigners, outsiders, so what does it mean that non-Jewish foreigners come to see Jesus? What do you think is the significance of gold, frankincense, and myrrh? What about the shepherds in Luke? Why shepherds? Go through each version slowly and discuss why the writer chose to tell the story in this way.

Here are some themes to keep in mind as you read these stories. First is that, in the ancient world, it was widely believed that great people's births were announced by heavenly phenomena, like an unusual star. Second, there is a tension in the gospels between Jesus carrying out his ministry for the Jews, of whom Jesus was one, and carrying out his ministry for Gentiles, or non-Jews. Third is that most of us scholars believe that there were questions about Jesus' identity and origins in the early years of the church, so a birth narrative may have served to help confirm that identity and those origins.

As you read and discuss all this, think about what these accounts of the birth of Jesus suggest about the importance of the poor and outsiders. Think also about what kind of king is born in such lowly, humble circumstances. Is this birth a rebellious alternative to the socio-economic and political structures of then and today?

My Suggested Bottom Line

The two accounts of Jesus' birth should be treated separately, but both tell of an event that challenges society.

Day Thirty-Four: The Sermon on the Mount

Reading: Matthew 5:1-12

Background

I heard a story of a pastor who got into the pulpit one Sunday morning and announced that he was going to preach the best sermon ever. He then read to his congregation the Sermon on the Mount.

I don't know if it's the best sermon ever, but it certainly is a masterpiece of Christian literature and one of the most influential passages in the New Testament. In fact, its influence has been felt beyond Christianity; Gandhi, for instance, who was Hindu, held the Sermon on the Mount in high regard.

It is called the Sermon on the Mount because, at the beginning of Matthew 5, the narrator tells us that Jesus goes up a mountain, sits down, and begins to teach the disciples. Going up a mountain is significant, because, in the ancient world, people associated mountains with the divine. If you wanted to be closer to God or the gods, you climbed a mountain. Where did the Greek gods live? On a mountain. Where does Moses receive the Ten Commandments? On a mountain. Where does Jesus go to impart his great sermon to his believers? On a mountain.

The sermon begins with what are often called the Beatitudes. They are statements that pronounce blessing (or happiness, depending on the translation) on those who are humble, meek, pursue peace, and strive to do right by God, even if doing so means being persecuted. The Beatitudes do not declare blessing for the wealthy, powerful, famous, and sexy.

The rest of the sermon, in many ways, elaborates on the Beatitudes by stressing how we are to treat one another. The sermon contains strict instructions on being loving, kind, forgiving, pure in thought, and not a show-off. The sermon also contains a version of the Lord's Prayer, as well as famous phrases such as "turn the other cheek," which challenges us to respond to violence with non-violent resistance. Some of the sermon will be hard for many of us to swallow, such as the condemnation of divorce except in cases of infidelity, or the idea that we should only worry about today. I certainly struggle with some of the sermon's teachings.

Discussion

Let's focus on the Beatitudes. What do you agree with? What do you disagree with? What would our society look like if everyone lived by the principles in the Beatitudes? Are they realistic?

My Suggested Bottom Line

The Sermon on the Mount challenges its readers to live according to the ideals of humility, meekness, peace, and love.

Day Thirty-Five: The Parable of the Good Samaritan

Reading: Luke 10:25-37

Background

S ometimes people say that Jesus always taught in parables. That's not true, but they do show up a lot in the gospels. He uses them often, just not always. In fact, John's gospel does not have any parables.

A parable, in this case, is an illustration that teaches us something about God and how to serve God. Jesus' parables are frequently shocking; that is, they surprise us with some sort of twist. Really, if you do not find a parable at least jarring, then you probably do not understand it.

One of Jesus' most famous parables is what is often called the Parable of the Good Samaritan, even though neither the word "parable" nor the phrase "good Samaritan" appears in the story. In any case, the story is so famous that the phrase "good Samaritan" has become both an everyday term and a legal term for someone who helps a stranger in distress. Jesus tells the story in response to a scholar of the law who wants to know what he must do to inherit eternal life. Jesus tells him to love God and the neighbor. The scholar, seeking to justify himself, asks, "Who is my neighbor?" Jesus then tells the story of a man on the road to Jericho who is robbed, beaten, and left for dead. A priest passes by him, not stopping to help. A Levite, an expert on the religious law, does the same. Then a Samaritan passes by but stops to take care of the person. That the person is a Samaritan is noteworthy because, in Jesus' world, Jews had little regard for Samaritans and did not associate with them. So then, it is shocking to have a Samaritan be the hero of the story.

The message, then, is twofold. First, who is our neighbor? Our neighbor is anyone in need, and we are to help her or him. Second, who acts as a neighbor to someone in need may surprise you.

Discussion

That a Samaritan would do the right thing would have been shocking to Jesus' audience. Who today would be shocking as the person doing the right thing? Instead of the Good Samaritan, what person do we not normally think of as good? The Good Politician? The Good Drug Dealer? The Good Terrorist?

Maybe there is some group that you are prejudiced against. For instance, if you are a Democrat, maybe you don't readily think of Republicans as good, or vice versa. This story is for you.

In the movie *Moonlight* (2016), Juan is a drug dealer who comes across a boy, Chiron, hiding from bullies. Juan tries to talk to Chiron, but he won't say anything. Juan takes Chiron home with him, where he and his girlfriend give him food. Eventually, Chiron starts talking a little. The next day, Juan takes him home to his mother, but a relationship has begun. Juan becomes a kind of father figure to Chiron. In one scene, Juan teaches him how to swim and also talks to him about being true to himself. When Chiron starts to wonder if he (Chiron) might be gay, Juan assures him that it is OK if he is.

Now, Juan never stops being a drug dealer. In fact, he deals drugs to Chiron's mother, much to Chiron's heartbreak. We in the United States generally do not think of drug dealers as good people, and of course, dealing drugs is a shameful profession. Even so, a drug dealer can still be a good Samaritan.

Who else?

My Suggested Bottom Line

The Parable of the Good Samaritan challenges us to think about how better to be a neighbor to others and also to consider that anyone is capable of goodness.

Day Thirty-Six: The Feeding of the Multitude

Reading: Mark 6:31-44

Background

The miracle of Jesus feeding over five thousand people is recounted in all four gospels. The details vary, but the basics are the same. Jesus has a large crowd of people in need of food, and he enlists his disciples to help feed them. That is, Jesus does not just produce food out of nowhere but calls upon his disciples to make a contribution. They offer five loaves and two fish, which are not nearly enough to feed so many. That's the point. Jesus then multiples that offering into a feast for all so great that there are twelve baskets of leftovers.

By the way, Jesus feeding bread to all these people gets many Christians thinking about Holy Communion, also known as the Eucharist or the Lord's Supper or the Last Supper. These terms refer to Jesus blessing, breaking, and sharing bread with his apostles the night before he died, saying, "Do this in remembrance of me." Jesus then blessed and shared a chalice of wine, saying again, "Do this in remembrance of me." This practice of Jesus has been done in countless churches around the world for two millennia and is generally revered as an important ritual that feeds both body and soul. In some denominations, most notably Roman Catholicism, the belief is that the bread and wine are the real body and blood of Christ.

There is endless debate about the details of Holy Communion. I am not going to get into that here. I will simply say that perhaps we can all agree that the ritual reinforces community and is meant to provide spiritual nourishment.

Discussion

Regardless of whether you believe that this miracle of feeding the multitude happened, it shows, among other things, how small contributions can produce greatness. Indeed, that's a theme in Jesus' teachings. The small mustard seed can become a great bush, a little bit of yeast can leaven a great amount of dough, and so on. Here, too, the meager contribution of the disciples ends up feeding thousands.

It is easy for us to think that our small contributions don't make any difference, but the reality is that the small can be the gigantic.

Kenyan Dr. Wangari Maathai, a biologist, observed that deforestation in the name of industrialization had caused severe environmental problems in her country, such as, for instance, greater erosion. Also, many women, who had relied on the wood for fires and housing and what-not, were now left without. To solve the problem, Maathai launched in 1977 the Green Belt Movement, which featured recruiting women to plant trees. The movement started small, of course. Maathai only had a few trees and a tiny group of volunteers. But the movement spread, bringing about better environmental conditions as well as jobs and resources for women. Maathai received the Nobel Peace Prize for her efforts in 2004, at which time some tens of millions of trees had been planted.

American journalist and author Dorothy Day was appalled by the plight of the poor during the Great Depression. With the guidance of Peter Maurin, she started a newspaper, the *Catholic Worker*, which highlighted injustice. She published the first issue in 1933, selling it for a penny. She and Maurin also opened a soup kitchen, even though they had little by way of money or other resources. Over the decades, they fed the hungry and housed the homeless while insisting on advancing non-violence, even when doing so meant losing subscribers to the paper. Day was repeatedly imprisoned for her acts of civil disobedience against wars and other acts of violence. Today, the Catholic Worker Movement has about 203 local communities providing assistance to those in need, the newspaper has a circulation of about 25,000, and Day is being considered for canonization.

Systemic change for helping the poor often starts small, even with one person, but can grow. Do not give up. And if it stays small, it still can make a difference.

My Suggested Bottom Line

The story of the feeding of the multitude reminds us how greatness can multiply from the small.

Day Thirty-Seven: The Death and Resurrection

Reading: Luke 23:32-47, 24:1-35

Background

For Christians, there is no more important event than the death and resurrection of Jesus. Christian theology teaches that this event is the central act by which God saves humanity—actually, all of creation—from eternal suffering and death.

However, the point of this book is not to try to convert people to Christianity but to bring people together through a focus on the strengths of the Bible that do not require a belief in God to accept. So then, with all due respect to the central claim of Christianity, I am going to move on to reflect on what in the story of Jesus' death and resurrection is of value for those who do not believe that Jesus is God or who do not even believe in God at all.

There is so much to say about the death and resurrection of Jesus that it seems silly for me to devote only one day of devotions to that event, but here I go. I chose for our readings a passage from Luke 23 that provides three statements that Jesus makes from the cross, at least according to Luke. First, he asks God to forgive those who have crucified him. Second, he promises one of the people being crucified with him that he will be in paradise with Jesus. Third, he commends his spirit to God; then he dies. After that, a centurion declares Jesus innocent, an important point given that he has just been executed for allegedly committing a crime.

For the resurrection, I chose to use Luke again, this time drawing from the first thirty-five verses of Chapter 24. There, we have women, not men, being the first witnesses of the empty tomb. Next, we have the touching story of the journey to Emmaus, in which the disciples don't recognize Jesus until he breaks the bread, an act that most of us scholars see as a reference to the Eucharist. Afterwards, the disciples rush back to tell the others what happened.

Discussion

Regarding these words of Jesus from the cross, what do they suggest about him? What lessons are embedded in them? Here is a man who is dying by crucifixion, and he still manages to focus on the welfare of others in two out of three of those statements. With his third statement, he turns himself over to God, thereby peacefully accepting death. So we have care for others and acceptance of death.

Of course, sometimes it is a tremendous struggle for us to care for others, and it is often a struggle to accept death. While this story challenges us to be better, it is not helpful if we come away from it being hard on ourselves for those times when we could not think of others or could not be calm about death. Frankly, there are times when we do need to put ourselves first; self-care is essential. But maybe these words of Jesus from the cross can encourage us, not shame us, to expand our capacity to care for others and to face death with peace.

What do you think? What do Jesus' words on the cross mean to you? What do you agree or disagree with?

Regarding the resurrection, there are several points worthy of discussion. One is simply the idea of life triumphing over death. The story of Jesus' death and resurrection is a story of renewal, rebirth, and revived hope in the face of lethal brutality. Death and evil wield their worst, and life and love prevail. How can this archetypal story revive and encourage you to keep going in the face of death? Where is there resurrection?

There's a saying: "It's Friday, but Sunday's coming!" When have you experienced Good Friday? How did you respond to that dark time? When did Sunday come for you? Are you still waiting?

Elizabeth Ann Seton loved her husband, William, and her five children. As a well-to-do American living in the early years of the United States, she absolutely adored being a wife and mother in her home in New York City, where she socialized with the Founding Fathers and Mothers. Then William's business collapsed, and he fell ill with consumption (tuberculosis). Desperate, she and William, along with their oldest child, eight-year-old Anna, traveled across the sea to stay with friends, the Filicchi's, in Italy in the hopes that the milder climate would be good for William's health. When they arrived, though, the Italians, fearful that William was carrying the dreaded yellow fever ravaging New York at the time, quarantined William and family in a dank facility called a lazaretto. During the month that the Seton's stayed there, William's health deteriorated. He died on December 27, 1803. Now, Elizabeth, at age twenty-nine, was a poverty-stricken widow, a mother of five young children, and an ocean away from home.

During her time in Italy—she was unable to journey home right away—the Filicchi's took her and Anna in. They introduced Elizabeth to Roman Catholicism, and she was so taken with the religion, that, once back home in the United States, she eventually converted, even though doing so meant being the victim of the strong anti-Catholic prejudice in the United States at the time. She went on to become a nun and found a religious order, the American Sisters of Charity of Saint Joseph, that would open a school, which was free for the poor, as well as an orphanage. Over the years, the Sisters spread their work to other cities and, eventually, countries. The Sisters have impacted millions of people around the world, and Mother Seton was canonized on September 14, 1975.

She experienced death and loss, but life and great gain emerged. She endured Good Friday, but Sunday came.

I often tell my students the astonishing story of Jean-Dominique Bauby, a forty-three-year-old editor of the French magazine *Elle*, who, on December 8, 1995, suffered a severe stroke. When he woke up twenty days later, he was essentially completely paralyzed and unable to speak. All he could do was move his head a little and blink his left eye. He remained that way until his death on March 9, 1997. He had been afflicted with locked-in syndrome, a rare condition that causes complete or almost-complete paralysis but that does not affect the mind. Bauby's cognitive ability was perfectly intact, but he was entombed in his body.

What did he do? He wrote a book. Claude Mendibil would read aloud to him the letters of the French alphabet, starting with the most commonly occurring ones. When she reached the letter he wanted, Bauby would blink. She'd write the letter down, then start over. Bauby and Mendibil worked this way four hours a day for ten months. It took about two minutes on average to complete one word, and the whole book took about 200,000 blinks.

When finished, Bauby had written a memoir about his life with locked-in syndrome entitled *The Diving Bell and the Butterfly* because his body was a prison like a diving bell while his mind was free like a butterfly. Just writing a book is an impressive achievement, let alone writing one in this manner. In addition, the book is eloquent, funny, poignant, insightful, and relatively free of self-pity.

Bauby experienced a death, but he also experienced a resurrection that led to a book of benefit to countless other people. It was Friday, but Sunday came.

Bauby died two days after publication of the book. He did not live to see just how influential his work would be, but Sunday came to him, even if only in a small yet profound way, through the writing and publishing of the book itself.

Another relevant discussion topic that we can derive from the death and resurrection story is the idea of life being with us and our not seeing it. In the Emmaus story in Luke 24, the risen Jesus is with the two disciples, but they cannot perceive that it is he. Their life and joy and hope are right there, but they are blind to his presence until he breaks the bread. Is it not the same with us? How often have we encountered life, love, or truth and not realized we had had the encounter until we looked back later? Many times we seek those things. Sometimes they are absent, but sometimes they are right with us if we have the eyes to see them.

Perhaps the power of a meal that we share with others can open our eyes. The breaking of the bread here seems to be a reference to the Eucharist, but could it not also be a reference to the revelatory power of meals in general? When that life, love, or truth is with us and leads us to a meal, that meal then may help us to see the life, love, and truth among us. Maybe? I don't know. What do you think?

American writer Raymond Carver has a short story entitled "A Small, Good Thing" about parents whose young boy dies from being hit by a car. Before his death, they ordered a birthday cake for him and then forget about it after the boy dies. The baker, who is eccentric, keeps leaving messages on their phone for them to come get their cake. He is rude and blunt and clearly does not know that the child is dead. Finally, the parents head to the bakery to confront this odd man. When he learns of their tragedy, he offers them cinnamon buns and then bread, which the three of them eat together. That's right; they break bread together. In that simple exchange, the parents are still heartbroken, of course, but they experience love in a small, good thing.

How can meals help us to see the love, life, and truth right in front of us?

My Suggested Bottom Line

The death and resurrection of Jesus can guide us to see hope and life and love in a world of despair, death, and hatred.

Day Thirty-Eight: Romans

Introduction to the Epistles

An epistle is a letter, and in ancient Greco-Roman society, letters were of high importance. Much of the New Testament is epistles, letters written to early Christians to guide them on how to follow this brand new religion. Thirteen of these epistles are attributed to Paul, a Jewish leader (a Pharisee) who persecuted Christians, regarding them as departing from the true faith, until he was converted to Christianity. According to the book of Acts, the risen Christ encountered Paul (also called Saul) on the road to Damascus, striking Paul blind in the process. Three days later, a Christian named Ananias healed Paul, who then converted to Christianity. Paul went on to become one of Christianity's most important theologians and evangelists. He founded congregations and wrote many epistles as a way of guiding his fellow Christians until he was executed in Rome sometime around 65 CE (remember that Christianity was illegal in the Roman Empire until 313 CE).

There is considerable doubt about whether Paul wrote all thirteen of the epistles that bear his name. It was common in the ancient world to put the name of a renowned person on your work, and that appears to have happened with six of these epistles: Ephesians, Colossians, 2 Thessalonians, 1 and 2 Timothy, and Titus. The other seven, Romans, 1 and 2 Corinthians, Galatians, Philippians, 1 Thessalonians, and Philemon, all appear to have been written by Paul himself. I could get into the details of this debate, but they are not relevant here. We can still arrive at some basic conclusions about our readings over the next few days even if we cannot agree on who wrote what.

There are other epistles in the New Testament not attributed to Paul: James, 1 and 2 Peter, 1, 2, and 3 John, and Jude. Hebrews, which is also not attributed to Paul, might be a letter, but it is structured more like a tractate or sermon. For that matter, some of the other books, such as 1 John, don't really resemble letters. The last book of the New Testament is Revelation, also not attributed to Paul. It has some of the features of an epistle but is ultimately what we call an apocalypse, which I will cover later.

Reading: Romans 8

Background

Paul's epistle to the Romans is his masterpiece. It is his most theologically sophisticated letter. He likely wrote it between 54 and 58 CE to a congregation in Rome that he had never been to. Sometimes Paul wrote to congregations he had founded or at least visited, but in this case he had done neither, although he was planning on visiting the Christians in Rome on his way to Spain.

Romans follows the conventions of Greco-Roman epistles: identification of the sender, identification of the recipient, greeting, thanksgiving section, body, exhortations, final greetings. The main topic of the epistle is what the church often calls "justification by grace through faith" or "justification by faith," which is a fancy way of saying that people get into heaven only through believing in Jesus and not through doing good deeds that earn a person her or his way to heaven. Paul argues that everyone is doomed, none of us can ever be good enough to make it to heaven on our own. The good news, though, is that we are saved as gift of mercy through Christ. We still need to do good deeds, because they are part of our new identity in Christ, but salvation is ultimately done by God, not by us.

Paul then shifts to the Jews who have rejected Christ. He contends that they, too, will eventually be brought to salvation and that their rejection of Christ was actually part of God's plan all along to get non-Jews, Gentiles, the opportunity to be exposed to Jesus and learn about how to get to heaven.

Chapter 8 comes about halfway through the epistle. It starts off by distinguishing between the way of the flesh and the way of the Spirit. The way of the flesh means the sinful side of humanity, while the way of the Spirit refers to the way of God. Of course, Paul encourages his readers to follow the latter, not the former. Note that Paul is not condemning the body. "The way of the flesh" is Paul's way of referring to the sinful inclinations of humanity and is not a condemnation of all things physical or pertaining to the body.

Starting with verse eighteen, Paul talks about the end of the world by basically saying that, while things are tough now, eventually all will be good. This redemption that we are moving toward will benefit, not just people, but all of creation.

The last nine verses are often read at funerals and emphasize the idea that, no matter what bad thing happens to you, nothing can separate you from God's love.

Obviously there is a lot of theology here that is distinctly Christian, but there is still plenty here that is of benefit to the non-Christian, as well.

Discussion

One topic to consider is the idea of the way of the flesh versus the way of the Spirit. If we think of the flesh as the part of us humans prone to doing bad and the way of the Spirit as the part of us humans prone to pursuing truth and love, then this idea of struggling between the two articulated in Chapter 8 has relevance to just about everyone. With that reading in mind, what advice does Paul give for helping us win the battle against our dark side? What hope does Paul give us?

Another topic for discussion from this chapter in Romans is about the importance of nature. Salvation is not just for people but for all creation. Romans 8 reminds us that this world is not only about us humans. A better future is something we should work toward, not just for people, but for every member of creation. We humans tend to think that we should care for creation because doing so will benefit us, but Paul teaches that creation will be redeemed for creation's sake and not just because of people.

A third topic is the idea of never being alone in the face of hardship. No matter what, you can always cling to Truth and Love even if you don't believe in God. Those qualities can persist with us even when evil howls around us, threatening to swallow us whole.

When he was in the concentration camps of the Holocaust, Jewish psychiatrist Viktor Frankl observed that people were more likely to survive if they had something to live for, some sort of why to make sense of the suffering they were trapped in. For him, at one point, that was the image of his wife. He did now know if she was even alive, but he fixated on her and the love between them to keep him motivated, to keep him from giving in to the cannibalistic world of madness roaring around him.

What is that Ultimate that keeps you going? It is never separated from you. It is with you always, even to the end of the age.

My Suggested Bottom Line

Paul's epistle to the Romans emphasizes the idea that we are saved by grace and mercy, that we are to persist in our commitment to good, and that we are never alone.

Day Thirty-Nine: Romans and Homosexuality

Reading: Romans 1–3

Background

Ugh, this is tough. One of the biggest controversies in Christianity is whether homosexuality is sinful and how to minister to the LGBTQ community. At the heart of this often hostile debate is what the Bible says about homosexuality.

Technically, the Bible says nothing about homosexuality as we understand it today. The word "homosexuality" never appears in the Bible, and there is no discussion of the viability of a loving relationship within the LGBTQ community. That said, the following passages are often cited as referring to homosexual behavior, and they are all negative: the story of Sodom and Gomorrah in Genesis 18 and 19 (where the word "sodomy" comes from), Leviticus 18:22 and 20:13, Judges 19:22–25, Romans 1:26–27, 1 Corinthians 6:9–11, and 1 Timothy 1:10. The passage that is the least ambiguous is Romans 1:26–27, which is also the only passage to mention what sounds like lesbianism. None of these texts adequately addresses the complexity of the LGBTQ community, including the mounting evidence that there is a strong genetic component to sexual orientation, that non-heterosexual people can be in loving, healthful relationships, and that a person's entire worth as a human being should not be reduced to what you or I think of their sexual orientation.

I am not going to get into the details of how to interpret these passages and whether they condemn the LGBTQ community as sinful. I contend that such a reading is simplistic at best and ignores the ambiguity of the language here and the significance of considering socio-historical context when interpreting a passage. I proudly belong to a denomination that ordains members of the LGBTQ community, but I understand that some of my fellow Christians, as well as non-Christians, regard the LGBTQ community as morally wrong. What I say to them is that it is fine to disagree with the LGBTQ community, but the nastiness and cruelty and bullying and vitriol are uncalled for and need to stop. All the viciousness is less about religious views and more about a deep-seated anxiety some people feel when they encounter members of the LGBTQ community.

Discussion

When we obsess over two verses in Romans 1, we miss the larger point of Romans 1–3 and, indeed, the book of Romans as a whole, which is that we all fall short and thus everyone is in need of salvation. So forget about homosexuality for a minute. Honestly, Paul could have left out those verses and still made the same point: Everyone is guilty. The point is not to lift up homosexuals as being horrible and to say, "Look how awful they are!" The point is to indict every person as falling short of the glory of God (3:23) and thus needing Jesus Christ.

For the non-Christian, the message could be that everyone needs help and that we are not to fixate on what someone else does wrong and thus ignore our shortcomings in the process. So then, even if you think someone is morally wrong, be sure to grade your own paper, and I'll do the same for me. Frankly, it makes more sense for me to look at myself and figure out how to improve myself, since I cannot control how others live. If I think I absolutely need to help someone who is doing wrong, it makes much more sense to do so with a spirit of humility than sanctimony.

How do you respond to people whose lifestyle you disagree with? How do we avoid being holier-than-thou? How do we help someone doing wrong while also being humble about our short-coming without berating ourselves?

My Suggested Bottom Line

Romans 1 through 3 contends that all of us have shortcomings and should not be used to justify cruelty toward the LGBTQ community.

Day Forty: First Corinthians

Reading: First Corinthians 13

Background

First Corinthians is my favorite of Paul's letter because the congregation he is addressing is a fascinating mess. It is obvious from this letter and 2 Corinthians that Paul and the congregation in Corinth have had a complicated and painful history of arguments and mutual mistrust. It is also obvious that the church in Corinth has a host of serious problems, from a man having a sexual relationship with his stepmother to people getting drunk during the Eucharist, to demoralizing rivalries over who has the better spiritual gift. In a desperate, eloquent attempt to save this congregation, Paul urges his readers in Corinth to focus on unity.

First Corinthians 13, the most famous chapter in the book, is to be understood in light of that quest for unity and ending disputes. The chapter, which never mentions God explicitly (at least not in the Greek; your translation might insert "God"), is a poetic meditation on love, one of the best pieces Paul ever wrote. This chapter is widely read at weddings, and that's fine, although it is not about romantic love per se but about the love God has for humanity and that people are therefore to have for God and one another. The Greek word for romantic love, "eros," is not used here; instead, we have the Greek word for selfless spiritual love, "agape," which, for Paul, emanates from God through Christ and is to be the guide for the lives of the Corinthians and, most likely, all Christians. The opening of the chapter, with its language about speaking in the tongues of mortals and of angels, is referencing speaking in tongues, a Christian practice popular in Paul's day and, among some Christians, today. Apparently members of the Corinthian church who could speak in tongues thought themselves superior to other Christians simply because of possessing that gift. Paul's response is that, without love, neither that gift nor anything else amounts to a hill of beans.

Starting in verse eight, Paul shifts to talking about the end-times, what we scholars call "eschatology" (the study of the end times). You see, in Paul's day, most Christians expected Christ to return from heaven any minute and for the world to come screeching to a halt so that a new, perfect existence could begin. In these last six verses, Paul is saying that, when that end comes, all these things that we think matter so much will be gone, but love will endure. It never ends.

Discussion

What guidance does this chapter provide us as we think about how to live according to this selfless love that we are to have for one another? Is the chapter saying that we have to like a person in order to love her or him? What is the most challenging part of this chapter? What is the most comforting?

Focus on verses four through seven, which describe love. What do you find helpful, shocking, upsetting, or reassuring about those verses?

Do you agree with Paul's description of love? Is something missing?

My Suggested Bottom Line

First Corinthians 13 is part of Paul's eloquent effort to stop the division of the church in Corinth and to get people to focus on this highest form of love instead.

Day Forty-One: Philippians

Reading: Philippians 2:5–11 and 4:4–13

Background

P aul's epistle to the Philippians is his most upbeat work. This is no letter to the dysfunctional, contentious Corinthians. Paul is happy with the church in Philippi. He warns them against false teachers and reminds them that suffering is part of the journey, but, on the whole, he is full of praise and encouragement.

Philippians 2:5–11 is likely from a hymn that Paul and his community would have known. Paul quotes that hymn the way many of us might quote a beloved song to make a point. In that hymn, often called the "Christ Hymn," Paul holds up Christ as a model of obedient, self-sacrificing humility and encourages his readers to go and do likewise. The key word comes in verse seven, when Paul says that Christ put aside his godly splendor and "emptied himself" so that he could serve. The Greek word there is a conjugation of a verb that means "to empty" and is connected to the noun-form, "kenosis." Christians often speak of Christ emptying himself and explore how Christians should follow suit.

Philippians 4:4–13 is one of the most beloved set of verses in all of the New Testament. Here we find hall-of-famers such as, "Rejoice in the Lord always; again I will say, Rejoice" (v. 4 NRSV); "And the peace of God, which surpasses all understanding, will guard your hearts and minds in Christ Jesus" (v. 7 NRSV); and, last but not least, "I can do all things through [Christ] who strengthens me" (v.13 NRSV). You can find these verses tattooed on arms and legs everywhere, and with good reason. They are inspiring, encouraging, and empowering.

Discussion

Regarding the Christ hymn and kenosis, what might self-emptying look like? What does it mean to empty yourself? In Philippians 2, the self-emptying is done in the name of serving others. When should we empty ourselves in the name of serving others? Are there times when we shouldn't self-empty? Does self-emptying have to do with putting aside selfishness for the sake of others?

Questions of his divinity aside, let's consider Jesus of Nazareth as a model, since that's what Paul is doing here. Jesus empties himself in order to obey God and save humanity by dying, but this act does not mean that Jesus was a doormat. Throughout the gospels, for instance, he is nobody's fool. He is caring, but he does not allow himself to be victimized. So then, where, for us, is the line between sacrificing ourselves for the sake of others and standing up for ourselves? How can we help one another know when to self-empty and when not to? Do we ever need to fill ourselves?

Back in my parish ministry days, I once used this passage as the basis for a wedding homily. I told the bride and groom that they would need to engage in a certain amount of kenosis, or self-emptying, in their marriage. In other words, in a successful marriage, as in every successful relationship, it's not all about you. There are times when you just need to put yourself aside for the sake of your partner. This act does not mean that your needs no longer matter; it just means that your needs are not the only ones that matter. There is an ongoing calibration, a balancing between self-needs and needs of the other person.

Kim and I have been listening to Michelle Obama's insightful and engaging memoir, *Becoming*, in which, among other things, she writes candidly about the challenges she and her husband have had in finding and maintaining happiness in their marriage. I have also listened to Barack Obama's *The Audacity of Hope*, in which he gives an account of their marriage that matches Michelle's. For instance, they both indicate that, early in their marriage, Barack used to work in a room alone for hours in the evening, leaving Michelle feeling neglected. He had grown up thinking that such behavior was acceptable and had to rethink what it meant to live with a spouse. He had to do a bit of self-emptying, which I imagine filled him in other ways. At the same time, Michelle has had to make huge concessions regarding Barack's political career, and they both continued to work on ways that Barack would keep being an integral family man.

Regarding Philippians 4, these verses encourage a positive attitude toward life by trusting in God. What or who empowers you to keep going? Maybe it's God. Maybe it's family. What enables you to keep rejoicing, finding peace, and being empowered? What gets in the way of those things? How can we keep rejoicing and finding peace when our world is so full of misery and every day life so full of monotony and stressors?

In *The Book of Joy: Lasting Happiness in a Changing World*, Douglas Abrams recounts a week he spent with Archbishop Desmond Tutu during his visit with his friend and fellow Nobel Peace Prize-laureate, His Holiness the Dalai Lama. One an Anglican Christian, the other a Tibetan Buddhist, these two men have been champions of peace for decades and are revered the world over for their wisdom. One of the arcing questions of the book is how these two men manage to remain so positive, even cheerful, despite the horrors and disappointments they both have faced repeatedly throughout their lives. A significant part of the answer that constitutes a major theme of the book is a heavy reliance on humor. Both men are well aware of how painful and miserable the world can be—the Dalai Lama has been in exile most of his life, and Desmond Tutu dealt directly with Apartheid in his native South Africa—but they both laugh deeply and often throughout their week together. The two sages stress that humor has repeatedly helped them to face adversity. Desmond Tutu speaks of once using humor to calm an angry crowd.

This emphasis on humor does not mean that we should be flippant or disrespectful in the face or difficulty. When I was a parish pastor, I rarely made humorous comments during funeral sermons. There is a time for seriousness, but a healthful sense of humor can help us to rejoice even when times are painful.

How do we do this? I recommend finding a person you can laugh with. Who shares your sense of humor? Whom can you joke with?

A person who is that for me is my dear friend Glenn. We have been best friends since we were roommates in college at Drew University. We have plenty of serious conversations, but we also excel at texting each other ridiculous statements. In fact, his humor (along with his calm, unflappable demeanor) helped me survive the first half of our first semester. You see, Glenn and I were not partiers (my idea of a wild night was two desserts), yet we were on a floor of all first-year students, many of whom thought we were ridiculous for not wanting to party. So they would get drunk and then, in the middle of the night, bang on our door. I hated it and got worked up about it, but Glenn was a rock. He just acted like it didn't bother him. He stayed calm, so I was able to, as well. Halfway through the semester, the bullying stopped. The dudes gave up and left us alone.

During that time and throughout our four years in college (1987–1991), Glenn would read to me the weekly Dave Barry column. With his ridiculous statements, Barry just cracked us up over and over. We still read him and talk about him today (and one time, in the name of being adoring fans, we sat in what we are pretty sure was his driveway).

Humor has helped me to rejoice, and perhaps it can help you, too.

My Suggested Bottom Line

Philippians 2 invites us to consider self-emptying in the name of serving others, and Philippians 4 challenges and inspires us to rejoice, have peace, and find strength in all circumstances.

Day Forty-Two: Philemon

Reading: Philemon

Background

At twenty-five verses, this is the shortest of Paul's epistles, but what a doozie! When he wrote Philemon, Paul was in prison, as he often was (again, Christianity was illegal), but because he's a Roman citizen, he generally received relatively pleasant treatment as far as prisons go. In this case, for instance, he was really under what was more like house arrest and so had some freedom.

We can glean from this epistle that Onesimus, a slave of Philemon's, has found his way to Paul, is staying with him, and, under Paul's guidance, has converted to Christainity. Paul is sending Onesimus back to his master, as the law requires, but first he is imploring Philemon to welcome Onesimus, not merely as a slave but now as a sibling in Christ. Paul gets a little manipulative here, such as when he says, basically, "you owe me, but I am not going to mention that" (even though he just did). Because of Christianity, Onesimus now has a new relationship with Philemon that he must honor.

There has been debate—this was a controversial book in the United States during the abolition controversy that eventually exploded into the Civil War—regarding whether Paul is saying that Onesimus should no longer be regarded as a slave or whether he still should be regarded as a slave who is also a sibling in Christ. Is Paul abolishing Onesimus's slave status? It's hard to say. In any case, at the very least Paul is recognizing that Christianity changes for the better how we treat slaves.

Discussion

What people in our society do we tend to regard as less than ourselves? How do we discriminate against people based on class, for example? Skin color? Sexual orientation? Gender? Religion? Can Paul's plea to Philemon to relate to Onesimus differently because of Christ translate into a plea for us to relate to one another differently based on Truth and Love?

One challenge for many of us is to be honest about our prejudices. We all like to think that we harbor no prejudice against anyone, but almost everyone is prejudiced against someone. Discuss with each other those prejudices and consider if Paul's letter offers any direction for how to relate to people we are prejudiced against.

My Suggested Bottom Line

In Philemon, Paul urges Philemon to treat slave Onesimus as a sibling in Christ.

Day Forty-Three: James

Reading: James 2 and 3

Background

This is not one of Paul's epistles, and in fact is not much like an epistle at all. As I indicated, epistles in that part of the world back then followed a careful structure that this epistle does not. We also don't know who wrote it. Is this James the brother of Jesus? Could be, but James was a common name back then. And, as we mentioned, the name on a document in the ancient world was not necessarily the author's. In any case, we have this whatever-it-is, this writing.

The content is a bit unusual in that there is almost no mention of Jesus, whose name only appears twice in the document. There is also no reference to much of the usual theology about Jesus, like that his death, resurrection, and return save humanity from eternal death. Instead, the document's focus is on how Christians should live. In this regard, James is somewhat similar in content to the Old Testament book of Proverbs, which also offers advice on how best to live. Chapter Two stresses the importance of not being prejudiced in favor of the wealthy and in opposition to the poor, and also urges readers to care for one another with meaningful actions. If, the chapter says in substance, we claim to have faith in Christ but do not have good works to go with that faith, then our faith is dead. If you're going to talk the talk, then you need to walk the walk.

Chapter Three warns against the tongue. We have all made hurtful statements; ancient people did, too. We need to be careful about what we say so that we do not cause a raging fire with one slip of the tongue. We all know this, but it is wise for us to keep reminding ourselves of this important truth.

Discussion

One worthwhile topic for discussion from James is caring for those in need and being welcoming to all. We have a tendency to favor the wealthy and to be wary of the poor. How is James helpful in guiding us against doing that?

This care for the poor reminds me of liberation theology, which was started in large part by Peruvian priest and theologian Gustavo Gutiérrez but now has spread throughout the world. Liberation theology argues that humans have created sinful institutions that contribute to oppression and that Christ is the one who leads people to dismantle those institutions and end political and socio-economic oppression. So then, Christianity becomes less about believing in Jesus to receive eternal life and more about imitating Jesus, who calls people to end oppression of the poor and marginalized. The book of James connects well with these ideas.

So then, what are ways we can help the poor that might make a more enduring difference? That is, a lot of our care for the less fortunate is relatively small and superficial, such as by donating a bit of money or food. Those gestures are important, but how can we contribute to systemic changes that can make it unnecessary to make those donations in the first place?

You might think that such an undertaking is too difficult, that we can't fight city hall. But remember little David defeating gigantic Goliath.

Regarding Chapter Three and the tongue, when was a time that you misspoke or someone misspoke to you? Why is it so hard for us to control our tongues? What in James can assist us in being "quick to listen, slow to speak," as it says in James 1?

My Suggested Bottom Line

The book of James provides ethical guidance on how to be kinder to another, especially the poor.

Day Forty-Four: Revelation

Reading: Revelation 13:11–18 and 21:1–6

Background

I included Revelation here because it is sort-of like an epistle. It starts off with the usual epistolary features, and it looks like it was circulated among at least seven churches. However, the book quickly turns into another genre: apocalypse, a word that comes from the Greek for "revelation."

Today, when we think of apocalypses, we tend to think of civilization-ending scenarios involving nuclear weapons or zombies, but back in biblical times, an apocalypse was a genre that used surreal imagery and symbolism to describe a significant end, what heaven is like, or both. Contrary to widespread belief, the book of Revelation is not necessarily about the end of the world but is merely about the end of the current age in which the book was written. The writer, John of Patmos, is offering hope and encouragement to the early Christians, who were enduring persecution. The book is essentially saying, "Don't give up. This present evil order will end, and better times are coming."

Christians are mistaken, then, when they regard Revelation as a detailed guide to how the world will end. The book is poetic and symbolic and so not meant to be taken literally and, again, is not necessarily about the end of everything but is about the end of the oppression that the Christians were experiencing at the hands of the Roman Empire.

In fact, Revelation is full of veiled references to the Roman Empire. For instance, the book mentions the evil city of Babylon, which was not a threat to Christians at the time that the book was written. Most of us scholars believe that "Babylon" is code for "Rome."

In Chapter Thirteen, which is full of strange and scary imagery of a dragon and two beasts, one of the beasts is associated with the number 666. There have been numerous explanations of this number. One I heard when I was a teenager was that 666 stood for President Reagan, who had six letters each in his first name, middle name, and last name. However, in ancient Greek and Hebrew, letters had numbers that they correlated with. When we apply that system, we get "Neron Caesar," or "Nero," a deranged emperor notorious for his sadistic persecution of Christians.

Revelation 21:1–6, which I often read at funerals, offers a vision of the new Jerusalem. In this vision, rather than people going to heaven, God and the new Jerusalem come down to humanity. Everyone will live together in a new heaven and a new earth. In this paradise, there will be no more mourning, crying, or pain. Further, we hear in verse five that God, right now, is working on making this utopia a reality. "I am making all things new," we read in verse five (NRSV). Times are horrible now, but the good new days are better by far than the good ole days. The best is before us.

Discussion

One fruitful discussion topic in response to Revelation 13 is to think about what makes someone beastlike. Instead of thinking that the beast, or antichrist as it is often called, is a one-time person, what if it's a type of person? The beast is deceitful; she or he makes you think that following her or him is good, but really doing so is going to destroy you. Do we ever see people who function in that way? Is that ever us? How can we respond to such people?

Of course, by using the term "beast" we are dehumanizing such people. Dehumanization is dangerous. Maybe the term "antichrist" works better. The point is that Revelation 13 is warning against manipulative, power-hungry charlatans. How does the chapter help us against such people? How does the chapter guide us so that we don't become like that?

Also, based on what you have read in the Bible, what advice does the Good Book provide for standing up to the Neroes of the world?

Revelation 21, too, provides fodder for discussion, such as: what can each of us do to help make the utopian vision of the chapter a reality? This is an ideal that the Bible puts forth; what can we do to make that ideal happen? Do you even agree with the ideal? What is your idea of a perfect society? Given what you have read in the Bible, what does it present as necessary for a utopian society, besides what we read in Revelation 21?

My Suggested Bottom Line

Far from being a guide to the end of the world, Revelation is an apocalypse that offers hope in the face of persecution and other hardships.

Day Forty-Five: Conclusion

How did it go? How were your forty-five days? Do you have a better understanding of the Bible than you did before? Did you do this alone or with others? Do you have a greater appreciation of the Bible as a work of literature?

What are some themes that recurred? One is certainly care for the poor. Another is love. Still another is that sometimes bad things happen to good people. Yet another is that the Bible is often negative toward women, but then there are interesting exceptions. And there is the Bible's built-in self-criticism.

I hope that this book has stimulated your interest in the Bible, regardless of your religion. The Bible is full of troubling passages, to be sure. Parts of it disgust me. But overall it is an extraordinary literary work that has much to offer and has been vastly influential. Therefore, the Bible is worth serious consideration.

Finally, I hope that my book can help to bring together people of different beliefs. Through Bible study, believers, non-believers, and everyone in between, can find some truths to agree on and increase their ability to work together.

It's time for a truce and then a lasting peace. I am weary of the either/or binaries of our nation. It's time for both/and. Believers and atheists and everyone in between can read the Bible fruitfully together.

I recommend that, for future Bible reading, you keep in mind the following ten principles:

1. A wise question about a given text is, "Why is this in the Bible?" That is, why did these ancient people think this needed to be included?

2. "What does it mean?" is generally a more productive question than "How did it happen?" Remember that something doesn't have to be factual to be true.

3. Overall, the Bible emphasizes love, helping those in need, and focusing on something greater than yourself.

4. The Bible is messy. We don't need to gloss over the messes, and we can still find value in the Bible despite them.

5. The Bible is self-critical and invites diverse opinions (to an extent).

6. At the same time, the Bible is not an anything-goes book.

7. If your reading of the Bible does not lead you to be a more caring, loving person, then you are missing the point.

8. The Bible should never be used to justify the oppression of others. We are all equal and should treat each other accordingly.

9. Beware of rigid, know-it-all approaches to the Bible. We don't know it all, myself included (I could be dead wrong about everything I've written here). Humility is always a wise approach to the Bible.

10. When we discuss the Bible, it's all right to disagree on interpretations. We don't have to convince the other person that they are wrong and we're right. There are often multiple valid interpretations of a text.

Next, if you are interested in studying the Bible further, I recommend the following. For the Old Testament/Hebrew Bible, I suggest the *Anselm Companion to the Old* Testament (Anselm Academic, 2014), edited by Corrine Carvalho. For the New Testament, I suggest Mark Allan Powell's *Introducing the New Testament: A Historical, Literary, and Theological Survey*, second edition (Baker Publishing, 2018). Both are thorough and scholarly yet accessible for a general audience. Also, they both have extensive lists of suggestions for further reading.

If you are looking for something more challenging, I recommend Steven L. McKenzie's *How to Read the Bible: History, Prophecy, Literature—Why Modern Readers Need to Know the Difference And What It Means for Faith Today* (Oxford University Press, 2009). This book is quite scholarly and gets deep into rigorous analyses of biblical texts, but it is worth the effort. McKenzie does a brilliant job of showing that many misinterpretations arise from contemporary readers not understanding the genres found in the Bible, such as when people incorrectly think that Revelation gives us a timeline for the end of the world.

Finally, if you are looking for a useful study Bible, I offer you *The New Oxford Annotated Bible*, fourth edition (Oxford University Press, 2010), which will give you information as you make your way through this long and complex work. I also recommend a study Bible based on Eugene Peterson's *The Message*, the fresh and thought-provoking paraphrase of the Bible I mentioned earlier.

Happy reading! And remember, the point is for us to come together. Yoke the disparate. Wouldn't it be great if reading the Bible did that?

Glossary

Abraham and Sarah: The progenitors of the Jews and, by extension, the Christians. Also, Abraham (called Ibrahim in the Qur'an) and Hagar are the progenitors of the Muslims. Judaism, Christianity, and Islam are collectively called the Abrahamic Faiths.

Apocalypse: A genre popular from about 200 BCE until about 200 CE that featured a dualistic world view of good versus evil, highly symbolic language, surreal imagery, descriptions of heaven, and accounts of the end of some major period or even the end of the world. The book of Revelation is an apocalypse.

Apostle: One of Jesus' closest disciples. Thus, all apostles are disciples, but not all disciples are apostles.

Baptism: The initiation, purification ritual for Christians involving water and invoking the Trinity.

Chosen People: The Hebrews, also called the Israelites, and later called the Jews.

Clean/Unclean: In ancient Jewish thought, some things and people are designated "unclean," not meaning that they are dirty but that they contaminate the clean and thus should be avoided. Two famous examples are pigs and people with leprosy, which, in the Bible, is actually an umbrella term for a variety of skin diseases and other contaminations.

Covenant: An arrangement between two parties. In the Bible, it is almost always a relationship God initiates with some or all of humanity. "Testament" is a synonym.

Epistle: A letter. The New Testament contains many letters.

Eucharist: A ritual in Christianity usually involving eating some form of bread and either wine or grape juice. It is also called the Last Supper, the Lord's Supper, and Holy Communion. According to Matthew, Mark, Luke, and 1 Corinthians, Jesus instituted this ritual the night before he died.

The Exile: The event in Israel's history in which the Babylonians destroyed the Temple and the city of Jerusalem, the capital of Judah (Southern Kingdom of Israel), and then took a portion of the population into captivity. The key year for this event is 587/6 BCE. It ended when the Persians, who had defeated the Babylonians, allowed the exiles to return home in 538 BCE.

The Exodus: The event in Israel's history in which the Israelites, under Moses's leadership, were set free from slavery in Egypt. This event includes the Ten Plagues and the parting of the Red Sea (actually the Sea of Reeds).

The Fall: Also called the Original Sin. The Christian term for the sin of Adam and Eve eating the fruit from the Tree of the Knowledge of Good and Evil.

Gentile: Someone who is not Jewish.

Gospel: Literally means "good news" and refers to Jesus saving humanity and all of creation from sin and death. The term also refers to an account of the life of Jesus. In the Bible, there are four gospels: Matthew, Mark, Luke, and John.

Israel: The nation of God's chosen people according to the Bible. In around 930 BCE, Israel split into two kingdoms. The larger Northern Kingdom was known as Israel, while the Southern Kingdom was known as Judah.

Jerusalem: One of the world's oldest cities, it was made the capital of Israel and then became the capital of Judah after the split around the year 930 BCE.

Judah (Southern Kingdom): The southern kingdom of Israel.

Judge: A political and military ruler in Israel before the monarchy was established.

Kenosis: Self-emptying. In Philippians 2:7, Jesus is described as having emptied himself in order to obey God by dying on the cross.

Messiah: Literally means "anointed one." The Greek-derived word "Christ" means the same thing. The term refers to a concept in the Old Testament/Hebrew Scriptures of a person God will anoint to rescue God's people. Christians see Jesus of Nazareth as the Messiah.

New Testament: The part of the Bible about Jesus and the early church.

Numbers in the Bible: Numbers are often symbolic. Recurring symbolic numbers are three, four, seven, ten, twelve, and forty. When you encounter one of these numbers, ask where else it shows up in the Bible and make connections. For instance, Jesus fasts in the wilderness for forty days, an act which reminds us of the Israelites wandering in the wilderness for forty years. Perhaps we are to connect those two events.

Old Testament: The part of the Bible about ancient Israel, before Jesus. For Jews, this is their scripture, and they often refer to it as the Tanakh. The term "torah" (which means "teaching") is usually used to refer to the first five books of the Tanakh, which are also the first five books of the Old Testament: Genesis, Exodus, Leviticus, Numbers, and Deuteronomy.

Pentecost: A miracle of the early church recounted in Acts 2 in which the disciples, by the power of the Holy Spirit, suddenly had the ability to speak in different languages.

Promised Land: According to the Old Testament, this is the land God gives his chosen people. Also called "Canaan."

Prophet: Someone who conveys a message from God to the people, usually a countercultural one.

Psalm: A hymn from ancient Israel used for worship in the Temple.

Sabbath: The day of rest and attending worship, which in the Bible, is sundown Friday until sundown Saturday (not Sunday).

Satan: Evil, anti-God figure in the New Testament. The Satan of the book of Job in the Old Testament is an earlier understanding of Satan as simply a member of God's heavenly court.

Second Coming: The understanding in Christianity that Christ will return at the end of time to judge humanity and defeat evil once and for all.

Stewardship: The term the church often uses to talk about humanity's dominion over creation. The idea is that humans are not rulers over creation so much as they are caretakers of God's creation.

Suffering Servant: The idea in parts of Isaiah of someone who suffers on behalf of others. Christians generally see these passages as referring to Jesus, but Jews offer different interpretations.

The Temple: The holy building of worship in Jerusalem in ancient Israel.

Theodicy: Explaining why, if God is all-powerful and all-loving, there is suffering.

Trinity: The understanding of the God of Christianity as being one god comprised of three "persons" (for lack of a better term): Father, Son, and Holy Spirit.

Wisdom Literature: An umbrella term for a group of writings in the Old Testament/Hebrew Scriptures that tend not to focus on Israel's history but instead feature guidance for a good life and an attempt to make sense of why suffering happens to good people.

YHWH: This is also often written as "Yahweh." It is God's name in the Old Testament/Hebrew Scriptures. It is considered very sacred. It is hard to translate but means something like, "He brings into existence whatever exists." The word "Jehovah" is derived from this.

The Bible at a Glance

This summary is based on the sixty-six books of the Bible that virtually all Christians agree are canonical.

Old Testament/Hebrew Scriptures (This is also the Jewish Tanakh, but the arrangement of the books differs)

Creation, Abraham and Sarah and Descendants, the Exodus, the Torah

Genesis
Exodus
Leviticus
Numbers
Deuteronomy

"Historical" Books

Joshua
Judges
Ruth
1 and 2 Samuel
1 and 2 Kings
1 and 2 Chronicles
Ezra
Nehemiah
Esther

Wisdom Literature and Poetry

Job
Psalms
Proverbs
Ecclesiastes
Song of Solomon

Prophetic Books

Isaiah
Jeremiah
Lamentations
Ezekiel
Daniel
Hosea
Joel
Amos
Obadiah
Jonah
Micah
Nahum
Habakkuk
Zephaniah
Haggai
Zechariah
Malachi

New Testament

Gospels

Matthew
Mark
Luke
John

"Historical" Book

The Acts of the Apostles

Epistles

(While the following are all categorized as epistles, some of them, such as Hebrews, probably are really some other genre.)

Romans
1 and 2 Corinthians
Galatians
Ephesians
Philippians
Colossians
1 and 2 Thessalonians
1 and 2 Timothy
Titus
Philemon
Hebrews
James
1 and 2 Peter
1, 2, and 3 John
Jude

Apocalypse

Revelation (somewhat like an epistle)

Bibliography

Abrams, Douglas with His Holiness the Dalai Lama and Archbishop Desmond Tutu. *The Book of Joy: Lasting Happiness in a Changing World*. New York: Avery, 2016.

Anselm Companion to the Old Testament. Ed. Corrine Carvalho. Winona, MN: Anselm Academic, 2014.

Bauby, Jean-Dominique. *The Diving Bell and the Butterfly: A Memoir of Life in Death*. Trans., Jeremy Legatt. New York: Vintage, 1998.

Carver, Raymond. "A Small, Good Thing" (1983). Accessed 30 July 2019. http://www.classicshorts.com/stories/sgthing.html.

Frankl, Viktor. *Man's Search for Meaning*. Boston: Beacon, 2006.

Gladwell, Malcolm. *David and Goliath: Underdogs, Misfits, and the Art of Battling Giants*. New York: Bay Back Books, 2013.

King, Martin Luther. "I Have a Dream." Accessed 30 July 2019. https://www.archives.gov/files/press/exhibits/dream-speech.pdf.

McKenzie, Steven L. *How to Read the Bible: History, Prophecy, Literature—Why Modern Readers Need to Know the Difference And What It Means for Faith Today*. New York: Oxford University Press, 2009.

Obama, Barack. *The Audacity of Hope*. New York: Random House Audio, 2007.

Obama, Michelle. *Becoming*. New York: Random House Audio, 2018.

Pope Francis, *Laudato si'* (2015). Accessed on 30 July 2019. http://w2.vatican.va/content/francesco/en/encyclicals/documents/papafrancesco_20150524_enciclica-laudato-si.html.

Powell, Mark Allan. *Introducing the New Testament: A Historical, Literary, and Theological Survey*, second edition. Grand Rapids, MI: Baker Publishing, 2018.

Schade, Leah. *Preaching in the Purple Zone: Ministry in the Red-Blue Divide*. Rowman and Littlefield, 2019.

Made in the USA
Coppell, TX
12 June 2021

57337969R00098